THE
Transgender
Manifesto

IAN THOMAS MALONE

The Transgender Manifesto by Ian Thomas Malone
Published by Green Muffin Publishing
Riverside, CT 06878
www.greenmuffinpublishing.com
Copyright © 2017 Ian Thomas Malone

ISBN-10: 0692954023
ISBN-13: 978-0692954027

Editors: Natalie Mooshman, William Brown, and Toni Rakestraw
Cover Design: Wicked by Design

Visit the author's website at IanThomasMalone.com

First Edition
Printed in the United States of America.

For Karl and Friedrich.
The future is ours.

CONTENTS

THE DAWNING OF A NEW AMERICA

B lessed are the queer, for we understand a truth lost on much of the world. A society beholden to a dated sense of normalcy, no longer. Recognition, that something upstairs does not compute with the shape of the external shell. A Big Mac cased in a Filet-o-Fish container. You know that presentation is half the battle. Everyone wants to feel comfortable in their own bodies.

Contrast that sensation with the idea of a standard method of doing things. The way your life is "supposed" to play out. Good grades, college, a job, a spouse of the opposite sex, kids. The white picket fence. Church on Sundays. A model of America, as it was once envisioned.

Not anymore.

There is nothing wrong with that way of life, if that is what you want. You being the singular identity that longs for this future. Not you, a plural collection of pamphlets designed to influence your soul's trajectory through retirement in Florida. Others can want this for you, but only you can make it work.

It won't if you long for something else, another way. The truth they don't want you to know about. There are other ways to be happy, even if there are those out there who would prefer if this were not the case. This book is for people on both sides of the equation, the beautiful and the damned. The heroes and the villains. The good witch, and the wicked.

If happiness was the only consideration, there would be no debate. The conservative ideology sees LGBT rights as an affront to the traditional way of life, for some reason. We are attacked as phonies, pretenders, even perverts, just for being who we are. There are people who wish for us to go back into the shadows, the closet, never to return.

Many of these people who wish to deny us our very legitimacy, who denounce us as mentally ill deviants, spend an hour each week paying homage to an ever-present, yet non-interventionist man in the sky. They go to courts across the land to defend their right to praise that uncorroborated deity at the expense of other people's civil liberties. To them, we the living, the transgender people who walk the earth, are fake, but the man up there, He is real.

One thing is clear. The only acceptable reason to go back into the closet is if you need to change your outfit. Social progress only moves in one direction: forward. We as a people, we as a community, we as a country, are never going back.

The transgender population represents the final frontier for accepted mainstream American hate, even as proxy wars are still being waged against women and every single minority group. At each turn, our society looked at what had been done before, and decided to chart a different route, at least on paper. America abolished slavery and gave women the right to vote. The courts even enforced gay people's right to marry, which did not even require a Constitutional Amendment. Only basic decency, but that was too much for a large chunk of the country, at least back in that distant era called the early 2000s.

The Transgender Manifesto

We will have our rights. The petty roadblocks thrown in our way, bathroom bills crafted in the name of "protecting the people," that only serve the politicians who seek to capitalize on the carnage created through their actions. There will come a day, maybe decades from now, when our nation will look back on this era with shame. After all the civil rights battles waged over the relatively short history of these United States, there are those who keep spinning the sick cycle of hate.

The list of demands is brief, even if the fight is complex. We want our rights, the ones that are apparently "God given." Jefferson's classic one liner, "All men are created equal," is supposed to have been recognized as extending beyond the original scope of white male property owners. America acknowledges where she's gone wrong without caring if the same mistakes pop up down the road, in the present and in the future. Sadly, many still face these issues on a daily basis.

A world where differences weren't used to strip full segments of the population from their basic humanity. Remember when our teachers taught us to share and to love each other, even though we don't all look the same? That notion is lost somewhere on the road between the kindergarten classroom and the real world.

Why?

The idea of a utopia where everyone has enough and no one suffers is a nice idealistic fantasy ensured to never exist in reality. Someone will always have more stuff than you. Likewise, someone will always have less stuff. Stuff being the key word, because we as a society can accept the notion of inequality based on material goods, even if we disagree with it.

We are not supposed to be okay with the idea of some people having more rights than others, not in the kind of abstract general sense that dominates any broad conversation on the state of America. That is not supposed to be what this country stands for. It is not until we specify whose rights are being called into question that people really start to move away from the notion of the shining city up on that hill.

The opening lines of Justice Anthony Kennedy's opinion in the landmark *Obergefell v. Hodges* decision tell us all we need to know about this silly debate. "The Constitution promises liberty to all within its reach, a liberty that includes certain specific rights that allow persons, within a lawful realm, to define and express their identity."[1] Seems like, according to the highest court in the land, we the people get to define ourselves, on our terms. Don't bother telling that to the right. They only like Justice Kennedy when he's on their "side."

As the war rages on, for the right to take a leak in the stinky public bathroom you feel least uncomfortable using, never forget this one fact.

YOU ARE LOVED
(IF THE BIBLE TELLS YOU SO?)

Transgender people are not cartoon characters. This is worth mentioning because for many, the jury is still deliberating, even as the rest of society has accepted the verdict. Those who seek to demonize us as freaks see what they choose to see, nothing more. You cannot change them, for facts are seldom as useful as we make them out to be. The mind can always override, change its course, if what's right there in front of it is unpleasant or undesired. The deniers prefer the wool resting against their eyelids.

Like the kindergarten classroom, organized religion spouts generalities that feel good to think about, like loving each other and helping one another out, in spite of our differences. God loves us all unconditionally, except for all the conditions.

There will always be people who question our existence, as if someone would embark on this journey for the kind of cheap thrills once found in Times Square back in the 80s. Infuriating, the idea that someone could look you square in the face and declare you an imposter. It is not okay, but it is not the real fight. Only a diversion, the undercard.

Never lose sight of the fact that love is out there, even if you do not feel it in your general vicinity. LGBT people have always had to look harder to fulfill the need for basic human affection. The road is often lonely, for reasons that do not have to exist.

The rejection of your identity by your pastor or your parents is not a rejection of you, the person. Only you as the image someone else wants you to be. That image will never make you happy.

WHO WANTS TO LIVE A LIE?

"Be yourself." One size fits all words of encouragement for any situation. Do you remember seeing any strings attached to that advice?

"Be yourself, unless you're transgender. In that case, don't be yourself."

Doesn't have the same ring to it. When faced with a choice between repression and authenticity in a general sense, the latter is always suggested. You'd think that if there was an exception to that rule in the case of transgender people, there would be a pretty good reason. If there is one, let's hear it. I sure can't think of any.

CONFUSED?
(LIFE ISN'T SUPPOSED TO MAKE SENSE)

Now, it is true that we do not know why transgender people are born the way we are, why our identities conflict with the designation assumed through our private parts. No one knows. That is okay. Sometimes it is good to embrace the unknown.

Really. Life does not make sense. Most animals live their lives eating or sleeping. Humans put on uncomfortable suits and take elevators to the sixty-seventh floor of the office building that houses their cubicles. We spend half our lives working even though a third of it is already spent asleep, ideally dreaming of scenarios that help us forget this painfully stale existence. If that doesn't work, there's always cocktail pharmaceuticals. We were not designed to be sensible organisms. We were meant to read Virginia Woolf.

People often point to the transgender identity as a mistaken attempt by otherwise confused individuals to explain their feelings. "You're not a woman, you're just confused," they say, with one hand on your shoulder as they try to push you back into the closet. Confused about what? What is this magical explanation that has escaped the millions of transgender people but is somehow known to these non-transgender purveyors of wisdom?

They don't know because they're not interested in solutions for transgender people. These people only care about preserving the status quo and all that it supposedly stands for (something else that hasn't really been explained). To them, transgender people are the problem. Confusion is their solution, not ours.

THE TRANS DENIERS ARE THE NEW BIRTHERS

The birther movement was a racist lie designed to denigrate President Obama. The topic was not discussed out of a legitimate fear that the rules governing America's democratic process had been circumvented by a Kenyan pretender. These people knew exactly what they were doing in attempting to obstruct President Obama's agenda by any means available. They speak with similar intentions on the subject of the transgender identity.

The motives: to undermine, delegitimize, obstruct. The success of their argument is not the objective because it cannot be proved. That does not matter as long as the debate carries on.

Once again they find themselves concerned with birth, and its subsequent ramifications. What the specific details of your birth say about everything that follows. A new era of birthers is born as America turns to the next chapter of this embarrassing saga.

"Your gender is defined at birth!" is their rallying cry.

To the birthers, being transgender is a decision that can be made with a snap of the fingers. "What if I decide I'm transgender?" they ask, ignoring the obvious answer to their ridiculous hypothetical. You cannot speak words out loud and have them construct your truth. Transitioning is a lot harder than that, though hard work is not something the birthers, with their lazy talking points, would know anything about.

Social media is a rich breeding ground for self-proclaimed experts on all sorts of subjects, including the legitimacy of transgender people. These often self-proclaimed "trolls" almost always lack medical degrees or decline to share their qualifications on a forum where their true identities might be discovered, yet never seem concerned by this lack of education on the subject. It is almost as if possessing a Twitter handle qualifies you to be an expert voice on any topic imaginable.

WE ARE NOT A FAD (WE'VE BEEN AROUND A LOT LONGER THAN DISCO)

Transgender people have been in North America longer than the United States. In 1629, Thomas(ine) Hall worked various jobs in Virginia, not adhering to the standards of either gender.[2] Hall was subjected to the same kind of cruel interrogation that still goes on today, only this humiliation was sanctioned by a court in Jamestown, who ordered Hall to wear clothing of both genders as "punishment" for the crime of causing public confusion. Society did not understand Hall, or simply did not care to find out. Who is to blame for that?

Chevalier d'Eon was a French solider turned diplomat who lived the second half of d'Eon's life as a woman after previously exhibiting androgynous traits and an ability to successfully pass as a woman when working as a spy in the Russian court. The French Court even recognized d'Eon's gender as female, requiring d'Eon to dress as such.[3]

There are some in American society who dismiss being transgender as a fad, akin to getting a nose ring or growing a soul patch. Something that young people want to experience, with the hopes of becoming YouTube stars or Instagram celebrities. One could point to many things to discredit this ridiculous idea, namely how preposterous it would be to undergo life-altering treatments because of a "trend," but there are better examples.

Thailand has the Kathoey. India has the Hijra. Samoan culture has the Fa'afafine. Polynesian culture has the Mahu and its variations. American Indian tribes recognize two-spirit people, including the Lakota Winkte, who exist outside the traditional binary. Much like America, these cultures have varying degrees of acceptance for their transgender people. Some are granted legal status, many are even honored, while others are considered to be at the bottom rung of their social ladder.

Transgender people are not a fad created by American millennials, much like how we're also not to blame for the rest of our country's problems. Today's climate is merely ripe for a long-awaited revolution. Efforts to dismiss us ignore the basic history of social science and put far too much faith in the logic put forth by online trolls.

THE BIRTHERS CLING TO THEIR SENSELESS TALKING POINTS

The superfluous clouds the need for substantial conversation. America loves to talk about the low-hanging fruit that captivates the mind's carnal instincts in the same fashion as reality television. The transgender platform takes a backseat to the juicier exchange of dialogue between two talking heads on cable news. We will not talk about health care, discrimination, or liberation if there's still someone out there willing to argue against our very legitimacy. That debate, full of insults and mockery, is always more fun to show on television.

This must change.

Prodding, they ask the questions that they know possess no tangible answers, not to achieve outright victory, but to delay the inevitable. We will have our rights someday. That day terrifies some people for reasons unknown. They do not want us around. That much is clear.

The people should be called what they are. Birthers, conspiracy theorists, followers of an antiquated view of the world. Name-calling may sound juvenile, but the title certainly reflects the maturity of the discussion. Plus, trans denier is a clunky term. Birther is far catchier.

THE LEGITIMACY DEBATE MUST END

The legitimacy debate is the single most toxic detriment to the furtherance of transgender rights. We can never advance the discussion if we must continue to fight for our legitimacy. This is by design, as the other side can never achieve its victory.

How can we be sure? Imagine the thought of a transgender person sitting at home looking at Twitter. A troll notifies this person that their biological reproductive genitalia defines their gender, nothing else. Does this person lean back in their chair, faced with the sudden realization that their entire existence has been based on a lie? This is

IAN THOMAS MALONE

part of the troll's prime directive, yet it is hard to envision it ever actually happening in reality.

This method of repression has been played out in every fight for equality. The origins of the "white savior complex" are rooted in the idea that the ruling class "knows better." Efforts to curtail every subsequent debate involve this similar "logic," that those who want their rights cannot be trusted to act in their own best interests. Women are "emotional," minorities are "savages," save for the few select "noble" ones, and gays cannot marry, for that would open up Pandora's box to subsequent chaos including, but not limited to, bestiality, polygamy, and incest.

We've seen this trick before.

None of these arguments are ever made using anything resembling logic for they are never made to serve logical purposes. Delegitimization is a last ditch effort by people desperately clinging to power. If you cannot offer a reasonable position to your opponent, make your opponent look unreasonable.

Opposition is delegitimized so that its side does not even need to be considered. The oppressors need that certainty so their rule is not called into question, inevitably exposing holes in this shaky logic.

Fortunately, the solution is simple. Stop tolerating the questioners. We should be done having that conversation by now.

The incomplete nature of the fight for transgender rights should not be seen as evidence that the legitimacy debate has not reached its natural conclusion. It has. The results are in.

WHAT DOES THE EXISTENCE OF TRANSGENDER PEOPLE SAY ABOUT THE "REALNESS" OF TRANSGENDER PEOPLE?

Transgender people exist. That statement probably doesn't do much to sway anyone's mind, but it does not need to be said for persuasive purposes. Only factual ones, because we know that transgender people are real. Saying so is simply a recognition of reality, despite what you hear on the internet and talk radio.

The most obvious evidence for the existence of transgender people is the existence of transgender people. You can Google "transgender" and see countless examples of transgender people. You are currently reading a book written by a transgender woman.

Now, I know it feels a bit cheap to define something using its own definition. Saying transgender people are real because there are transgender people will not convince anyone who denies our existence. And yet, doesn't it prove something?

You can point at a cloud and say it is a cloud without needing to explain why it isn't a satellite or a giant piece of fluff caught in the troposphere. I wouldn't recommend pointing at transgender people in public as a means of identifying them, but you could see a transgender person and acknowledge them to another individual, who would be able to understand what you were saying. This is not an abstract concept.

This person could, in theory, refute you and say that the transgender person is faking and that they are actually a different gender, one they may have been assigned to at birth. That does not change the fact that both people saw a transgender person and were able to identify them as such. One just wanted to be an asshole about it. The difference is not as important as you think.

There will come a day when fewer conversations about transgender people are held with that obnoxious addendum attached. Enough people will recognize transgender people as what we are (people), that subsequent discussions regarding legitimacy will neither be held nor tolerated.

The Biblical story of Doubting Thomas comes to mind. Thomas did not believe until he had physical material proof of Jesus' resurrection. Trans people can supply that evidence just by existing. Of course, if that were all it took, we wouldn't be having this discussion.

It is as if they don't want actual evidence.

WHAT IS "REAL," IN THE ABSENCE OF A STANDARDIZED TEST?

The central argument against transgender rights is that we are all faking it. We're playing pretend, indefinite dress up, and would like the government to officially sanction this charade, so no one can rain on our parade. That is what the opposition would like you to believe.

That we should not have rights because we are not real.

This opinion is quite popular on the internet, all across the broad landscape ranging from the mainstream social media to the more intimate troll lairs. You can hardly even mention the word "trans" in a public outlet without someone expressing this sentiment, believed to be backed by logic. If you give the strings of sensibility just a teensy little tug, you may find that the whole blanket falls apart in the face of this one question:

What is real?

The lack of an official transgender test serves as a rallying cry for the birthers. If it cannot be proved, it must be fake, according to this rationale. This is spoken despite the accepted existence of plenty of other things that cannot be verified to be real with a simple yes/no test.

WHAT ABOUT THAT THING CALLED FAITH? WHAT'S THAT ALL ABOUT?

What is faith, if not an acceptance that there are things out there that cannot be explained?

You know what you know, because you've never lived a life without that truth. That you are different, that your gender did not compute with that label assigned at birth. It does not matter how large a percentage of the general population is perfectly fine with their identity. That does not change you, how you responded to the mechanisms that made you who you are.

It is not in question. The people who pressure you back into the closet operate under a false illusion, that this is all a façade. They believe that tens of millions of us across the world are lying, all playing pretend because we are diseased perverts dissatisfied with our wardrobe options at the mall.

Deny, deny, deny.

Who are they to know? What business is it of theirs anyway? These people who vote for candidates running on the platform that the government does not belong in your private life, asserting their infinite wisdom over your domain.

I pose this question again because it is an important one. How do they know?

These people always seem quite sure, beyond any doubt, that they are correct, that transgender people are imposters, phonies, fakers. They display similar faith in their own beliefs, though they cannot offer any proof to defend these positions.

What is religion if not mankind's attempt to explain the unexplainable? Even if we accept the basic gist that there's a celestial being out there who put us all here for some reason, billions of people have to have gotten almost all the specifics wrong. The differences in the creation stories among the major faiths ensures this. Yet people still believe and continue to fill places of worship around the world, fully aware that plenty of other people are doing the exact same thing for a completely different faith.

The Transgender Manifesto

We as a nation accept that billions of people across the world worship an isolationist man in the sky, who never intercedes in times of war or natural disaster, but still has a set of rules that He wants us to follow if we want to go to His clubhouse, also located in the sky, after we die that no one still on earth has had a chance to visit. No part of heaven has ever been made available as an Airbnb, even though there are a few people on earth could probably afford the transportation.

You can say that description is slightly irreverent, which it is, but I still accept that billions of people believe this stuff. It just makes you wonder why so many struggle with the very real, very tangible existence of transgender people, here on earth. Maybe we should send a transgender person to the Moon.

The absence of a "transgender origin story" or any kind of abstract consensus as to why we're here on this earth should not be used against us. No one else can explain the broader odd quirks of humanity either. Why we sit at desks all day staring at cat pictures on our phones when we could be home with actual cats. Why Oreos and peanut butter taste so good together. Why we need Netflix, Hulu, and Amazon Video when other species get by without any streaming services at all. We don't know the answers to any of these questions.

It shouldn't be held against us. We have our places of worship. They differ too. Some of us like going to Sephora, others to MAC.

WE GIVE "FAITH" RIGHTS

Our currency reads "One Nation Under God" despite the fact that no Founding Father ever proved that the United States of America is situated beneath a supreme being. We accept that our coins are not imprinted with fake news even though we've seen no evidence to the contrary.

Unlike being transgender, you do get to choose your religion. Our country has laws protecting all religions, even the ones that have historically caused conflicts. The term martyr exists because people are killed often enough for their religious beliefs that it warranted its own word. Martyrs *chose* to believe in something that ended up getting them killed. That of course does not excuse a single crime committed against someone because of their religious beliefs, but it does make you wonder why transgender people should not be afforded the same protections just to live our lives peacefully, as we are.

No religion had to prove that it was real before the First Amendment was passed, which accomplished two main objectives with regard to religion. The First Amendment ensured that no religion would be favored by the government over another and that the government would not interfere with a church's right to conduct its business, within reason. Various interpretations as to the specifics of those two broad assertions form much of the legal precedent that has followed in the subsequent centuries.

The First Amendment established clear lines for where the government wanted to get involved with regard to religion. The basic parameters established that people could believe whatever they want, as long as it does not violate the law. Most court cases involving religion tend to focus on what constitutes a violation of the law, ranging from polygamy to bakeries. Somehow, transgender people and the LGBT community as a whole got wrapped up into this mess.

"Live and let live" seemed like a great mantra for many early immigrants who came to America to flee religious persecution. It is generally a great mantra for all people to follow, except for all the strings attached. You see, many religions don't want transgender people to live and let live. They want us to live somewhere else instead.

DID GOD MAKE US AS FINAL PRODUCTS?

Religious people often condemn trans people over the whole surgery aspect, using fiery words like "mutilation" to contrast our decisions with God's supposed intentions for humanity. The trouble is, while the Bible doesn't mention transgender people, it does have some words about body parts and certain circumstances that might call for some modification.

"If your hand or your foot causes you to stumble, cut it off and throw it away. It is better for you to enter life maimed or crippled than to have two hands or two feet and be thrown into eternal fire." (Matthew 18:8)

There is a lot to unpack here. I don't go to church much, but I don't see many missing body parts around the congregation when I do make an appearance. Now, we can say these words are meant in a figurative sense, but then that opens them up to interpretation. Like this one:

"If you suffer from gender dysphoria, transition. It is better for you to live life happy than to have a fully functional reproductive system and be thrown into eternal fire." (Ian 18:8)

See how easy that was? Is my version really that much different from the original? Still has the same avoiding eternal fire gist. If God really thought transgender people were going to hell, He might have wanted to have been a little more specific.

There are also a lot of gray areas that do not have anything to do with transgender people. Tonsils, appendixes, spleens, cosmetic surgery, ear piercings, shaving, nail clippings, etc.

Some might argue that some of those are more okay than others. Fine, but that's not the point. To say God doesn't want transgender people to have surgery is picking and choosing, unless you are not on board with any of the aforementioned bodily modifications either.

That also ignores one simpler truth. If you look at those words from the Book of Matthew, it is certainly possible that God does want people to transition. The words do pretty much spell that out. If it's going to be open to interpretation, those anti-trans religious folk should at least admit that they might be wrong. Good luck with that.

MR. GORBACHEV, TEAR DOWN THIS BINARY

The binary crumbles every time a man or woman participates in an activity typically designated for the opposite sex. From the macro subjects like workplace equality, to the smaller achievements like the male romper, we as a society are slowly learning that male and female are labels best not painted on with a broad brush, unless the color is pink and the template is a man's fingernails.

We've only had jeans for women since the 1960s. There's a lot of work left to be done. So many new possibilities.

Why do we allow these rules to govern our behavior? Society in the present tense governs over it, but no one living on this earth created the binary. We only exist in its reality.

Tear it down.

If a societal norm serves no purpose, cast it aside. There's an easy way to figure this out. Ask yourself, does this serve a purpose?

Some might worry that this would lead to anarchy where people ran around naked flinging their junk around. I don't think so. That's what the question is for. You see, if you asked yourself whether going to work in your birthday suit was a good idea, you would hopefully come to the conclusion that it was not a good idea because you would get cold from the office air conditioner, among other reasons. The system works.

The binary will come crashing down, one unnecessary

societal behavior at a time. Time has already made its mark on these dated "rules" of societal conduct. Re-read *Pride & Prejudice* if you don't believe me. How many rules in that "book of manners" survive? Some, but not all. Society asked itself some questions.

WHERE LIES THE BURDEN OF PROOF?

If a birther says trans people are a made up hoax and transgender people say that we are not pretenders, who has to offer the proof? The answer to this question may seem tricky since it is unclear what the stakes are in a theoretical example, but this is a topic debated at every level of the fight for equality, from the online trolls to the halls of Congress. Theoretically, this nonsense could all be over if one side could offer unquestionable evidence to prove the other side wrong once and for all.

Let's put aside the fact that the birthers would likely never be convinced for any reason, which presents a whole different problem. Think back to middle school, the preferred environment for these trolls before the dawn of the internet, where name calling could be uttered in public with little fear of repercussions. If you had a medical reason that prevented you from participating in gym, what did you need to show to get out of it? Perhaps a doctor's note? Schools tend to accept those without needing further absolute proof that there's actually something wrong with you, or that the illness was not something you "chose" to have.

The idea of a doctor's note proving anything about

transgender people sounds fairly preposterous. If that's too much of a stretch for you, we can take a step back and go one by one through the things it does prove for transgender people on hormone replacement therapy (HRT). For starters, it shows you are serious and have thought about this stuff for longer than a single evening while you looked at Tumblr. It shows you have consulted with medical professionals, who presumably have not only thought about this stuff, they have studied it too.

What kind of work has the birther put in to contribute to this discussion? This question is a bit more abstract, given that it is impossible to construct an accurate profile of the average troll. Some birthers are obviously more informed than others.

Transgender people have demonstrated that we engage with this subject on the substantive level required to make life-altering changes to one's body. The birthers have shown that they can repeat the stale "your gender is defined at birth" talking point. While that may not prove much to skeptics, it does show where the actual stakes in this debate reside. That has to count for something.

HOW CAN YOU KNOW (AND REALLY BE SURE)?

You already do. How's that for a wishy-washy answer? It's true. Therapy and doctors can reaffirm that reality, but you know who you are. If you're not sure, think some more. It'll come to you, eventually. Or it won't, and that's kind of an answer too.

The more important question is: what are you going to do about it? Keep living the lie, or embark on a long and difficult journey? The right answer might be obvious, but that doesn't make it easy.

There is no reason this decision needs to be as difficult as it is. The only factor should be you. The way you see yourself. It isn't. Society butted in, making its opinions known. There are a lot of loud voices who want to weigh in, urging you to pick repression, not out of your best interests, but their own selfish desires.

You'll know for sure when you stop asking yourself the question. The outside noise can delay that process, but not indefinitely. We should not forget that the noise does not belong in the conversation at all. This is your decision, your identity. Drown out everything else. You won't be happy until you do.

"STATES' RIGHTS" STRAW PEOPLE

States' rights is a complex topic. It is often used as a defense by people opposed to LGBT rights, even after the outcome of *Obergefell v. Hodges* shattered this silly argument.

The Tenth Amendment was included in the Bill of Rights for a good reason. "The powers not delegated to the United States by the Constitution, nor prohibited by it to the States, are reserved to the States respectively, or to the people."[4] You see, back then people were worried about the federal government becoming an unwieldy overbearing leviathan, unlike what it is now. States' rights offered the kind of self-governing protections that formed the basis of the ideology behind the Declaration of Independence.

States' rights make sense when you think about things like taxes, given that states have different individual economies. There are rational reasons for why taxes in Texas are different than taxes in Rhode Island. It makes less sense when you think about matters like segregation, marriage, and bathrooms.

Since the 1960s, the term "states' rights" has essentially become a dog-whistle rallying cry for the implementation of government sanctioned discrimination against women, minorities, and LGBT people. Some might disagree with that notion. To them, I pose this question:

Why would a person need to use a different toilet in Alabama than the one they use in California?

We're not talking about taxes, only toilets. There is the idea that the specifics are not important, only that the state has the right to impose its own laws. But then where does the "or to the people" come in? What about civil liberties?

There is a place for states' rights in the conversation for how to successfully govern a country as large as America. We are, after all, the United States. I don't think our Founding Fathers, flawed as they were, started a war for the right to let states decide which latrines its people could use. One would think there were bigger issues at hand. I'd like to think that state governments have bigger concerns than bigoted bathroom bills. If that's what they spend their time doing, maybe "states' rights" as a concept is not so important after all.

BATTLING THE TRANSGENDER STRAW PEOPLE

Given that actual transgender people are not to blame for the current state of America, the birthers design transgender straw people to battle instead. These creations are typically monsters who wait in bathrooms, locker rooms, and elsewhere looking to prey on the innocent, non-trans population. LGBT people face these hypotheticals all the time. They repeat variations of "if we give them rights, then this horrible thing will happen and America will be over."

It won't.

Gay marriage has been around long enough for society to tell if it has led to an increase in people trying to marry their dogs using this same "anything goes" logic that people on the right warned was imminent. It hasn't. Likewise, transgender people have been peeing in bathrooms long enough to tell if there has been any increase in transgender-related bathroom sex crimes. Again, the data is missing.

Too many ideological battles are fought using reactionary warfare. Bad behavior is excused by pointing to someone else's crimes. The fight for equality is countered by bizarre theoretical scenarios that never seem to actually end up existing in reality. This back and forth is apparently easier than facing real issues affecting real people, but it's nonsense and we should not be expected to put up with it.

If someone poses a ridiculous hypothetical to you, follow it down the rabbit hole. Play it out. Spell out the nonsense until it is so painfully obvious that the person feels stupid for ever having asked the question. Granted, there's a chance this person may not be reasonable, having already demonstrated evidence pointing to that conclusion, but you never know.

Talking points often sound like facts when they're repeated enough over a long period of time, even when they can be easily debunked after spending a few minutes with the old noggin. Spend that time. Engage the opposition, forcing them to do the same. So much of the hate against LGBT people is based on ridiculous logic. Time to expose it.

THE PANOPTICON OF THE PHALLUS

The ever present power of the male genitalia. Isn't that the real reason some people cannot accept the existence of transgender people, transwomen in particular? Men, who can't begin to fathom that there are some people out there who do not thrive off the mystical power of testosterone. Explains why most of the online trolls seem to be men.

Transwomen further represent the living contradiction of this rejected universal truth. It may be hard to believe, difficult to comprehend, uncomfortable to consider. Your teeth may grit as you read this, but that does not make it untrue.

Not everyone wants to have a penis.

The trouser snake, lurking in the garden of the fruit of the loom. The power it believes it holds over the general population. The freedom to exert that power, without fear of consequence.

"Boys will be boys."

We're taught to like bravado. The cool kid, the rebel, the one who dared to stand out. Whether we like it or not, every other element of the human identity exists in relation to this shining Calvin Klein model on a hill.

Mad Men's Don Draper is championed as the gold standard of workplace masculinity. Women who exhibit similar behavior in the office are criticized, mocked as "ice queens" or advised to "smile more" if they want a promotion that would otherwise be awarded on merit, if sexism did not feel an obligation to play its role.

The false standard that governs over masculinity hurts all of us, especially those who do not fit its mold. Transgender women are seen as freaks because some people cannot understand why anyone would not want to have a penis, or be filled with the hormonal energy produced by the wonder twins. The latter is actually more important.

There is a distinction between not wanting a penis, and actively hating it. Not all transwomen undergo bottom surgery for many reasons, one of which stems from a lack of desire. Despite the mind's natural affection for topics relating to penises, it is not even a requirement to transition. Many state courts will allow you to change your gender on your birth certificate without undergoing sex reassignment surgery (SRS), not that the government has a great track record with handling these issues.

I get that it is weird for some people to accept that a person could have a penis and not be completely in love with it. This notion can stir all sorts of emotions within a person, including many of Freud's favorites. It is okay. Some things do not need to be understood, though the world would be better off if the penis was kicked off its totally non-phallic pedestal.

I'll let you in on another secret. Many transwomen do like penises, including their own. That might be too much for some brains to handle. That we come in many shapes and sizes, and likewise, enjoy many shapes and sizes. If you doubted the power of phallic imagery over your mind, re-read the previous sentence. What did you see?

For thousands of years society has measured men by the bravado exerted by their testicular region. This once universal standard is crumbling after centuries of siege by those who see no purpose in the forced exertion of a dated gender norm. Some people may fawn after that golden calf, but we should no longer see it as the standard for what it means to be successful. There are other ways to live your life, freed from the always present prison warden, keeping watch from his perch in your underwear.

WHAT IS THE VALUE OF AN APPENDAGE?

To the birthers, the physical presence of a penis or a vagina is crucial. The only thing that matters.

We as a society don't discuss whether or not men who have orchiectomies, or women who undergo hysterectomies or mastectomies, cease to be their respective genders, if they do so for medical reasons other than being transgender. There are many great reasons not to have that conversation. The notion itself is cringe-worthy enough.

But many of the presented arguments against transgender people put all their stock into the value of appendages, so they do kind of have to be worth something. Some might note the distinction between those who were born with these parts and those who weren't, except this train of thought starts to cross over from fact into feeling territory, especially if we're strictly judging whether something is or isn't there. The appendage either has value or it doesn't. It's not a checkpoint.

There are also the people who are actually born without penises, or ovaries, or all those other parts that supposedly determine gender. What do we make of them? A birther might acknowledge that intersex people represent outliers compared to the general population, which is true. Transgender are also outliers, but that does not mean we aren't real.

REMEMBER THE UNISEX BATHROOM?

The popular 90s television program *Ally McBeal* continues to inspire debate, usually related to the titular character's complicated relationship with feminism, which led to an infamous 1998 *Time* magazine cover. You know what wasn't so controversial? The show's unisex bathroom, complete with remote controlled flushers and dance sequences to the music of Barry White.

While several characters expressed discomfort over the

theatrics that went on in that bathroom over the course of the series, no one ever expressed concern that they might be sexually assaulted by a transgender person in a single episode. No one on the show ever wondered if transgender people should be forced to use a separate bathroom from the unisex one. I guess you could say that might be because the show was a comedy, but transgender issues have been used for comedic purposes for hundreds of years. Just ask Shakespeare.

It is worth mentioning that transgender people were less visible in the 90s than we are today. That does not mean we weren't still there, still using the bathrooms. Funny how the bathroom bills and the military bans didn't pop up until more of us started coming out of the closet. It's almost as if that was the real concern!

WHAT DO THE COURTS SAY ABOUT THE BATHROOM DEBATE?

Whose duty is it to cast formal judgment on the trans legitimacy debate? The courts come to mind, especially the case *G. G. v. Gloucester County School Board*.

The following is a brief summary of the key points of the case,[5] which is still ongoing at the time of this book's publication. Many major news outlets, including *The New York Times* and *The Washington Post*, have extensively covered Grimm's story. Their reporting is highly recommended for further reading.

Gavin Grimm is a transgender man who was prohibited from using the boys' bathrooms and locker rooms at his high school while he was a student. The lawsuit only came after the school board passed a policy banning transgender students from using the bathrooms and locker rooms that corresponded with their gender identity. Previously, Grimm had been allowed to use the boys' bathrooms by the school's principal for over two months before the new policy had been approved.

The case was first dismissed by the district court under an interpretation of Title IX in July, 2015, before being overturned by the United States Court of Appeals for the Fourth Circuit in April, 2016. The Supreme Court stayed the decision made by the Fourth Circuit in August, 2016, and had agreed to take the case in October of that same year, before reversing that decision in March, 2017, following modifications made to the guidelines of Title IX by the Trump administration.

What is particularly relevant in this case is that the presiding judge, Robert Doumar, did not even initially accept that Grimm was male, referring to him as female in court. Judge Doumar also described being transgender as a mental illness and admitted to having decided the Title IX argument before evidence was presented. To be fair, judges are human, though this truth always complicates the idea of a genuinely impartial judiciary. After the Fourth Circuit ruling, Judge Doumar issued an injunction allowing Grimm to use the boys' bathroom, though not the locker room, pending the outcome of the case.

While Grimm's school hardly treated him with the

basic respect that any student should receive, they had initially allowed him to use the boys' bathroom, later offering single person unisex bathrooms as an alternative when the school board objected. I note this not to suggest that the school deserves praise for any of its actions, but rather that the school never tried to argue that Gavin Grimm is female. The only person who did try to claim he was female, Judge Doumar, later issued a ruling in Grimm's favor.

This is a debate over Title IX, not the legitimacy of the transgender identity. The distinction may not matter to many, since Grimm is being discriminated against for being transgender, but it does speak to the overall weakness of general arguments against transgender people. No one makes the claim that he's faking his identity, yet they still press forward with these hateful measures. The fact that the school does not want to touch the issue of the legitimacy of the transgender identity further solidifies the broader bathroom debate's status as a proxy war used to legally sanction discrimination.

The role of politics in this case is undeniable. The only reason the Supreme Court refused to take up the case is because the Trump administration had revoked earlier federal guidance issued by the Obama administration, which had been cited in the Fourth Circuit's ruling. Nothing else changed. The eventual ruling, if we ever get one, will reflect politics much more than the realities of the case. Chief among them being that Gavin Grimm is male.

It is important to note that this entire legal debate is over the rights of a teenager to use a school bathroom.

This case has visited multiple courtrooms, costing quite a bit of money, all because a school won't let a brave student exercise his rights. It is nothing short of disgraceful.

If all men are truly created equal, Gavin Grimm should never have had to go to court to fight for the right to use the same bathroom as every other member of his gender. The fact that this case is still ongoing, years later, after Grimm graduated high school, is a stain on the moral fiber of this nation. That principle of equality was supposed to be self-evident. Guess not.

WHO GETS TO DECIDE WHO GETS RIGHTS?

I actually have an answer for this massively broad question. Clearly the courts have their limitations, but there is a simpler judge and jury. The public.

The role of women in society has changed drastically over the past hundred years. The role of women in society has changed drastically over the past twenty years. You can expand or shrink that number however you want and see similarly cosmic alterings of the ever-present binary. This doesn't happen by accident. Time plays a factor in swaying public perception, but people cause these changes. They will continue.

There is a reason politicians go after LGBT people. Unfortunately, there is a segment of the population that likes this kind of stuff. There is also a segment of the population that may not necessarily like bathroom laws, but is not going to change their vote because of discriminatory policies.

The results of North Carolina's gubernatorial race demonstrate the power of this issue. Of the twelve states that held gubernatorial elections in 2016, only three elected governors of a different party than that of the candidate the state cast its Electoral College votes for in the presidential election (North Carolina, Vermont, New Hampshire). North Carolina saw incumbent Republican governor Pat McCrory defeated even though the state went for Donald Trump as well as incumbent Republican senator Richard Burr. Of the three states that voted for one party's gubernatorial candidate and the other's presidential candidate, McCrory was the only incumbent governor seeking re-election. Incumbents are typically pretty difficult to unseat.

It isn't really an oversimplification to suggest that McCrory lost strictly because of North Carolina's Public Facilities Privacy & Security Act (also known as HB2 or simply, the bathroom bill). Most polls over the past hundred years show that upwards of 90% of people vote for one party on a ticket. Split ticket voting is rare in general, but an article by Amber Phillips of *The Washington Post* noted that it was historically sparse in 2016.[6] Yet it happened in North Carolina.

President Trump's recent actions banning transgender people from the military can make it easy to forget that he largely stayed away from LGBT issues during the campaign, even at one point telling *The Today Show's* Matt Lauer that Caitlyn Jenner could use any bathroom she wanted at Trump Tower on April 21st, 2016, though he later reverted to the mainstream Republican stance of the issue being a matter of those pesky "states' rights."

The failed re-election of Pat McCrory does demonstrate that this issue has power. Most politicians' number one fear is a poor turnout at the voting booth. If human decency is not enough to stem the tide of these stupid discriminatory laws, a strong message from the ballot box might do the trick. If you hate these laws as much as I do, fear not. They can be defeated. We can be the change we want to see.

THE HANDEDNESS VARIABLE

Most people are right-handed. Less than 10% of the world's population, myself included, are left-handed. We don't choose, either way. Left-handedness is not made up, in case you weren't sure.

This may come as a surprise, probably not, but the topic of handedness' effect on identity isn't really talked about all that much. There's plenty of science regarding brain hemispheres and whatnot that suggests it could make a major impact on who we are as people, but we have no way of gauging that. It is just something that is.

The creative sectors of my brain that possibly explain my left-handedness could also be the reason why I love the movie *The Tree of Life*, even though I don't think I actually love *The Tree of Life*. Or, 35% of the reason why I like the color magenta. Or 67% of one of the thirteen reasons why I think glazed donuts are delicious. We don't know and we probably never will know.

The transgender identity functions in a similar way. You cannot isolate its impact because it has always been a part of you. With regard to who you are, it is anything and everything, simultaneously. The ones who point at you as pretenders for not being able to explain why you are the way you are could never answer that very question for themselves. The only difference is that we don't typically ask that question to the general public.

MUCH ADO ABOUT CHROMOSOMES

We hear this one a lot. "You're born with XY chromosomes. You're a man. You can't change DNA." Usually followed by something about biology.

Let us, just for a second, take in the fact that many of these people who use this logic are the very same folks who denounce climate change as a made up hoax. For them, science only matters when it can provide evidence in their favor. Fortunately, this is something we can work with.

Science class teaches us that men generally have XY sex chromosomes and women have XX. They don't always. There are other options. There's XXY, XYY, XXX, XXXX, XXYY, XXXY, XX/YY, and so on. No one knows how many combinations are out there, but there's definitely more than two.

A birther could try to argue that different chromosome patterns do not matter as long as the transgender person in question has either XX or XY sex chromosomes. According to them, having XX, or XY denotes either female or male. Problem is, it can't. If that were true, the XXY person would be a different gender, something more specific than simply "intersex" to distinguish this person from someone with XXYY sex chromosomes. For the birthers' logic to be sound, there would have to be quite a few genders. I don't think that's what they had in mind.

"Intersex" is a term that can fit under the transgender umbrella depending on the individual person's own preferences, but generally refers to people who were born with sex chromosomes, reproductive organs, or genitalia typically associated with both men and women. Birthers tend to dissociate them from the rest of the transgender community because their existence further complicates the notion of there only being two genders. Living proof of a world without a strict overbearing binary created by a man in the sky. I'd say irrefutable proof, but the birthers seem pretty intent on doing their best to ignore all the facts right before their eyes.

This is a messy subject that calls for greater scientific analysis than yours truly is qualified to provide. Scientists do not have a consensus as to what exactly chromosomes tell us about gender identity. The logic that uses chromosomes to delegitimize transgender people is about as sound as the science that supports those supplements you see on late night infomercials or the stone eggs that Gwyneth Paltrow's company tells you to put in your vagina. Sex chromosomes do tell us one thing. There's definitely more varieties than your typical XX or XY fare.

THE FALLACY OF THE MENTAL HEALTH ARGUMENT

I see a lot of birthers who suggest that trans people need help for so-called mental health problems. While I have no doubts as to the impurity of their motives, they're not really wrong. Talking to someone about this stuff is a good idea, certainly not something to be mocked. I certainly benefited from therapy.

There are a lot of stigmas surrounding mental health as well as those who speak to therapists, who are themselves derided as "shrinks." This clouds the fact that therapy is very beneficial to a large number of people. That's kind of the point of the word therapy.

Strip apart the "get help" insult used when people behave in manners outside of the accepted norm for whatever social setting they find themselves in. "Get help" is used in plenty of non-ironic circumstances, like when someone has been in an accident. Help is supposed to be a good thing.

Referring to transgender people as basket cases ignores the fact that we as a group do benefit from therapy to help us understand who we are, not necessarily who the world wants us to be. Most people would if they sat down and shared whatever was bothering them. It isn't good to keep things bottled up. Transgender people all have that really big secret we kept hidden, for however long it took each of us to come out. That secret can tear someone apart. If it is actively causing harm to an individual, getting help is a pretty good idea.

We need to destigmatize therapy because mental health is a major concern for the American public, transgender or otherwise. We as a nation do ourselves a great disservice pretending it isn't. Those kinds of conversations inevitably raise broader concerns about the state of the health care system, but they are important to have. Lives are at stake.

The people who say transgender people should get help are onto something, despite their best intentions. They also might want to take their own advice, especially if something internal is driving them to spend large portions of time spreading hate on the internet. Something is clearly bothering them. Take it from me, get it off your chest. Life is better when you're not keeping stuff bottled up.

BUT WAIT! NOT ALL CONSERVATIVES ARE BIGOTS

I imagine there are people who are offended, or may claim to be offended, by the notion that there is a correlation between conservative ideology and an opposition to LGBT issues. There is. Some may call that an overgeneralization, which it is, since not all conservatives want to deny LGBT people our basic rights.

Two words for that: Boo hoo.

No one should feel sorry for that overgeneralization. Mainstream conservative outlets offer platforms to birthers of many kinds, including those who spout ill-conceived transphobic hate. Why should we be concerned about the "good ones" when we don't tend to hear them voicing opposition toward the people responsible for sullying their "good" name?

You want a pass? Earn it. These anti-transgender laws are wrong. Speak up, or forever hold your peace, while people like me hurl proverbial feces toward your general vicinity.

I know not all conservatives are bigots. You know that too. This is why we have this section, where this fact is acknowledged multiple times. Now we don't have to burden the rest of the book with precursors like "some" or "not all," every time the political right comes up. Painting with a broad brush is bad in a general sense, but not really in this one if the people who tolerate the bigots are also a problem. The non-bigoted conservatives are really just mad that they are not being differentiated enough from the birthers. As a certain orange president might say, sad!

I can't help wondering why conservatives love talking about transgender people so much, even when they criticize liberals for doing so. Is it because they genuinely think we're ruining the country? Are they really concerned for our well-being when they call us confused pretenders? What's the end game? Why keep talking about us, if not to rally support from a sector of the population that definitely does not care for us?

Mainstream politics tolerated the Ku Klux Klan a few decades back. That should not be forgotten either. The sins of the past can be explained away, but what about the sins of the present? Some may reject the notion that oppressing LGBT rights falls under this category, just like people did back then. History is not going to be kind to the losing side of this argument. Repression never wins in the long term. The conservatives who take umbrage with my categorizations would be wise to remember that. They dismiss the LGBT population for overwhelmingly voting blue without ever stopping to consider why this happens.

SUPPOSE THE BIRTHERS ARE RIGHT

I'm comfortable enough in my own identity to present the question of what might happen if it turned out transgender people were not, in fact, real. Which presents an interesting question.

What does that change?

Legally, it changes quite a few things. It allows trans people to be discriminated against at will. Fired for wearing the clothes on their body. Denied services for any reason that could possibly fit under the banner of "religious liberty." The establishment of a caste system, where some Americans finally get to feel the way they've always wanted to feel:

Superior.

Is that what we really want? Is that where we really want to go, as a nation? Framing this subject through the "what does it matter if they have rights?" question does not feel appropriate given the stakes at hand, but we should consider the question of why people care so much about the simple idea that trans people should be afforded the same rights as anyone else. Ask them and they'll point to examples like expensive medical procedures. Let's take a look at that.

THE "COST" OF HEALTHCARE

Ha. That is what should be said to anyone who expresses a serious concern about the cost of transgender-related medical issues affecting the health care costs of rest of the general population. Say it with me again. Ha.

That fallacy is nothing more than a MacGuffin. A bright, shiny object for you to look at, and to consider as a reasonable argument, distracting you from being concerned about anything else. On the surface level, the logic seems to add up. Having sex reassignment surgery is more expensive than not having sex reassignment surgery.

Same goes for, you know, cancer. Or diabetes. Epilepsy. A lot of really bad diseases that require expensive medical treatment over long periods of time. The American health insurance market would be a lot less expensive if no one in the country had any of the preexisting conditions covered under the Affordable Care Act. We would not even need health insurance if no one ever got sick!

And yet, people do get sick. Some people are born transgender, and therefore require certain medical care that people who are not born transgender do not need. You don't buy health insurance because you know you're going to get sick. You buy it because there is a chance you might, and if that happens it would be very expensive if you had to pay for everything out of pocket.

Kind of like what trans people have to do if they don't have insurance plans that cover certain procedures. Or at all. The people who say trans people should not be covered by health insurers are often the same who say we should not be protected from employer discrimination. Employer provided health insurance remains the most popular form of coverage in the United States.

In other words, there are people who do not want trans people to have health insurance, or protection from discrimination at a job that would enable us to pay for our own expenses. Our public discourse does not connect those two opinions enough, even though they are essentially one and the same. I'd say we're lucky the people who feel that way are not in charge, but Congress is hardly reassuring on that front. The question of what they actually do want for transgender people is not posed often enough. It is not a stretch to say they quite literally want us to die, given that they don't want us to have access to any kind of medical care at all or the money to do so for ourselves.

You would think that buried in all that anger for the money spent on transgender medical care, there would be an underlining concern for the growing cost of healthcare in general. Premiums are, in fact, rising. People struggle to pay their bills. These burdens are not caused by transgender people. There are not enough of us requiring significant surgical procedures to make a sizable impact on the bottom line. Remember, not all trans people get bottom surgery, which is by far the most expensive transgender related procedure.

If you have insurance, transgender hormones are not very expensive. Mine only cost a couple bucks a month, which is a drop in the bucket compared to a lot of daily medications. If you don't have insurance, the prices go up exponentially, but that is not a predicament unique to transgender people.

Imagine how cheap those pills would be if we could figure out the whole issue of the rising costs of prescription drugs. Again, not a uniquely transgender related issue. We don't belong in some separate category. These facts may not matter to people who just want someone to blame, but we as a nation should not have to take them seriously.

"But wait!" an objector might say. "One does not choose to get cancer. The transgender people are trying to scam the American people with their pretend condition."

We as a community should be more okay with this line of thought than the idea that transgender related care is too expensive a burden for the healthcare market. This rationale lays its cards out on the table properly, for all to see. I have no problem with them trying to make that argument as it demonstrates that their true motives do not lie with a desire to improve health care, but rather to carry out a malicious assault on transgender people. It all goes back to the sense of superiority. We shouldn't have to take this idea seriously. It should be filed under the "too bad if you don't like it" category of nonsense that intelligent adults don't have to entertain. Because, again, being transgender is not a choice.

We as a nation do not really love talking about the concept of personal responsibility with regard to health care, even though we know that certain habits increase one's risk of illness. Singling out transgender people based on the idea of a choice is not just wrong, it is hypocritical. Birthers may not care about being wrong, but who wants to look like a hypocrite? Is being transgender really more of a choice than picking up that pack of smokes at the gas station? To them, it might be. After all, cigarettes are quite addictive.

People who do not want transgender people covered under medical insurance do not carry these sentiments out of a legitimate feeling of grievance. They cannot tell you the effects that transgender people have on their premiums. Instead they point to an abstract idea, that transgender people cost more money, that while true, is not going to fix the healthcare market. Maybe try focusing some of that anger on actual solutions.

BY WHAT AUTHORITY ARE YOU DOING THESE THINGS (MATTHEW 21:23)

You may question my qualifications to speak with authority on such a complex subject. While it is true that I have spent precisely zero hours working in the health care industry, this should not disqualify me for the task at hand. I'm not trying to fix health care. I'm not sure Congress is either, for that matter.

Our public discourse does not dive into the specifics. We float around the generalizations, sailing around in a never-ending circle. Some of us would really like to break that cycle because we're tired of being blamed or scape-goated for bullshit that can be easily debunked, if one only sits down long enough to think about it.

It is easy not to think about things in today's climate. Cable news airs five minute segments that ensure no one could possibly have a substantive discussion, with the con-stant bickering serving as an additional deterrent. Twitter overloads the mind with more daily content than even a supercomputer could possibly process. Snapchat embraces the ephemeral moments that disappear within seconds of first contact, even going so far as to notify the sender if a recipient broke that code by taking a screenshot.

The trouble is that trans people need certain things to get thought about. There's a lot of nonsense out there. Fake news, as some might call it. Ideas about trans people that go unchecked, even if much of it can be debunked if one were merely to spend five minutes following this "logic" to its natural destination.

Ignorance is dangerous. Trans people know that bet-ter than many. The decision to undergo hormone replace-ment therapy has significant medical ramifications and as such, is never taken lightly. I don't even need to write, "should never be taken lightly," because no trans person makes that choice on a whim, despite what anyone tells you.

THE DYSPHORIA DILEMMA

The World Health Organization declassified gender dysphoria as a mental disorder in 2014 for a surprisingly simple reason. The meeting of the minds[7] that led to this change argued that gender dysphoria did not meet the criteria for a mental disorder on the grounds that the dysphoria alone did not necessarily cause distress. Rejection of one's identity, whether from society or the individual, is a much more prevalent cause of distress or anxiety related to gender dysphoria.

In other words, gender dysphoria is not a mental illness because it does not cause mental illness.

Granted, a person who does not possess feelings of gender dysphoria is unlikely to feel distress related to gender dysphoria, but this is not a cause and effect relationship. A transgender person who feels depressed because her parents told her she was a freak is not feeling depressed because she is transgender. She is upset because her parents told her she was a freak. The fact that she would not have been rejected if she was not transgender is not relevant. Crap like that is called victim blaming for a reason.

Self-help books often call for people to look inward toward themselves for acceptance. This advice isn't very helpful when it comes to gender dysphoria. Self-acceptance is important, but it's also nice to live in a world where people don't hate you just for being who you are.

HRT SAVES LIVES

I would know. Certainly saved my life. Which is not to say that testosterone is poison that takes lives, but it sure didn't sit well in my system.

There are many who would dismiss the positive feelings after HRT as psychosomatic, as if a placebo could achieve the same effect. This theory is debunked through decades of medical studies on HRT, but I have a few bits of my own evidence to offer.

HRT is not some magic pill that cures all worry. I've had bad things happen to me since the first needle was injected into my right butt cheek. My hormone pills have not shielded me from any concern over anything wrong in my life. Instead, they've allowed my mind the clarity to handle each punch as it comes and to react accordingly. No more "sky is falling" fears over minor setbacks.

HRT is a medically administered treatment to an ailment. You take aspirin when you get a headache. That doesn't mean all your worries for the rest of time magically melt away when you wash down the pill. Only that you don't have to face the world with a blistering headache.

Countless transgender people can attest to the benefits of HRT. In theory, that should count for something, as should the numerous medical studies conducted on this subject over the past few decades. Apparently, the birthers know better.

LET THEM EAT CAKE
(UNLESS IT'S GAY WEDDING CAKE)

NIMBY (Not in my backyard) found a cousin in the bathroom bills and the gay wedding cake debate. The idea of equality for all Americans is nice, in the abstract sense. In practical life, not so much, not when there's all this "religious liberty" to defend. A new acronym is born, that conveniently applies to both topics.

NIMSB: Not in my straight bakery/bathroom.

There is some practical wisdom to offer those bakery owners who do not wish to provide cakes for gay weddings. Come up with a believable excuse. Figure out a way to decline the request that does not reveal your true motives. Don't expect the government to provide one for you.

Here's another idea. Stores open to sell products. Bakeries make wedding cakes, to sell wedding cakes. If someone comes in wanting one, make them a cake. Don't sit there and try to come up with a parallel example, like if a Nazi came in wanting Nazi wedding cake. That's stupid. Nazis don't come in asking for wedding cake. If that happened, Fox News would have covered it for an entire month.

WHAT ABOUT THE TESTS ON THE INTERNET?

There are tests on the internet that claim to tell you if you are transgender or not. This is a load of nonsense, but that does not mean these tests do not have some sort of practical value. Personality tests like the kinds you find in fashion magazines often simply reaffirm what you already want to believe.

Only the individual can truly know, but the individual needs to feel confident in what they actually know. There's plenty of inspirational movies where young students expect old mentors to bestow ancient powers upon them, only to find that the real magic comes from within. These tests don't bear much in common with Mr. Miyagi or Rafiki, but they can serve a similar function.

Understanding one's identity is a process that cannot be completed through a test you found on Tumblr. That test can reaffirm your instinct that something is up. You wouldn't be taking it otherwise. In that regard, they do have value. Just not in many others.

OUR SUICIDE RATE IS WAY TOO HIGH

There is a cost to this discrimination. Lives are quite literally at stake. Almost all studies place the transgender population's suicide rate at several times higher than the general population.

It breaks my heart every time I think about it. All the beautiful souls we've lost, continue to lose, as society entertains the stupidity passed off by right wing trolls as substantive policy discussion. Their hate is sick, and it carries real world consequences. They bear blame for every suicide within the LGBT community.

Some may call that unfair. I don't think so. While it is true that the choice to take one's life ultimately lies with the individual, there are plenty of external factors that drive one to this decision. Discrimination creates seemingly insurmountable barriers, especially when coupled with an outside world that tells you your very existence is an abomination. The mind can take itself to some pretty dark places when it sees nowhere else to turn.

Too often, society tells transgender people that we should turn to those dark places, after doing its best to take all the other options off the table. Again, the loudest voice in the room can be very difficult to ignore, especially when you're already beaten down by everything that life has thrown at you. It does not need to be this way.

Transitioning liberates us from these dangerous emotions, in spite of the birthers' constant nattering, using right wing media's megaphone to point us back toward the darkness of the closet. Life does get better. We must never lose sight of that. Nor should we forget that there is no good reason transgender people should have to ever experience this level of rejection in a seemingly civilized world.

Our suicide rate will go down as the world becomes more accepting of transgender people. The birthers who deny that they've ever played a role in this needless carnage will undoubtedly point to other reasons. They can never wipe the blood that's already been shed from their hands, but we will not forget the souls we've lost as we fight for a future where none of us ponder that fate for ourselves.

If you're reading this and are currently experiencing those feelings, know this. You are not alone. It may feel that way, but it's not. Trust me, I've been there. Don't give up trying, even if your initial efforts are in vain. There are many LGBT organizations dedicated to fighting this battle. Help is out there. It is so gut-wrenchingly awful that we have to try this hard to feel okay, but that fight will always be better than the alternative. Always.

Life doesn't need to be this hard for us. Someday it won't be. Let's try for that, today.

ON POPULATION FIGURES

There are certain people, usually on the political right, who argue that we should stop talking about LGBT issues because the topic is disproportionately discussed relative to how many of us there actually are. Many studies estimate that transgender individuals account for about half a percentage point of the U.S. population.[8] Not exactly a big number, even if we accept that it is difficult to gauge population figures when many transgender people are still in the closet.

What to make of that? In hypothetical scenarios, it might seem plausible to try to argue that we as a nation spend too much time talking about LGBT issues. Pundits on outlets like Fox News argue that the reason the Democrats lost in 2016 was because they spent too much time talking about transgender bathrooms and not enough time on the economy. Once again, transgender people find themselves scapegoated, this time for taking up too much of the public conversation.

The biggest issue with the screen time argument is that over the past two years, the media has often has spent over 90% of its time talking about one man, even when the consensus opinion was that he had 0% chance of ever being elected into a position of power. Donald Trump himself accounts for far less of a percentage of the population than transgender people. You might think that there are flaws in comparing one politician to an entire community and that is certainly true, for many reasons. Chief among them being that we spend way too much time talking about Donald Trump. Dissecting the legitimacy of how the media spends its time is a losing proposition. It isn't meant to be fair.

The idea that transgender people are in the news simply reflects the fact that topics related to transgender people constantly create news. Bathroom bills are controversial. Controversy creates news. I'm not really sure how transgender people could be responsible for the media coverage of President Covfefe's vague tweet that banned transgender people from serving in the military. Then again, the birthers seem to be pretty good at blaming us for all sorts of things. I'm sure they can come up with an excuse for this one too.

Many studies estimate the size of the Jewish population at between one and two percentage points higher than the transgender population in America. While that single percentage point accounts for millions of people, it's a drop in the bucket relative to the rest of the population. There are far more than 1% more Jewish CEOs and Supreme Court justices than there are transgender CEOs or Supreme Court justices. If that comparison seems odd to you, it's because it is. Again the concept of comparing what amount of representation is fair for minority groups feels strange, because it's a discussion that we are not used to having. It only seems to pop up when a scapegoat is needed.

We spend a disproportionate time talking about minority segments of the population because they are also the ones who receive a disproportionate amount of the oppression. We talk about these people because their rights, and in many cases their lives, are at stake. A simple solution for these people who want to talk about something else would be to stop trying to take these minority group's rights away. Seems too obvious, doesn't it?

WHAT IS DESIRE?

To be content, to be distracted, to be whole. Broad definitions for a deeply intimate feeling. Not because other people can't see what you want, but because you can never be fully sure why your mind has selected its desires. To you, the reason you love the things you love, like sports, art, books, etc. feels natural, unexplainable. But there is a reason lurking there, even if you are not quite sure what it is.

We gravitate to where our talents lie because of a feeling of completeness that stems from seeing the fruits of that labor. You lose yourself in that which you love because it makes you feel okay, in spite of whatever else is going on in your life that might otherwise be troubling.

I've always felt that way when I write. Before I transitioned, writing offered an escape from the reality I'd inevitably have to return to. The desire to write remains even after HRT eradicated its value as a distraction from the life I didn't think I could have. I can't fully explain it, and that's okay.

Desire manifests itself in many forms. Think about what it means to "have it all." "All" is just a collection of a bunch of different desires. A job, family, good health, a 401k. You didn't set out in life with only one desire, unless that one desire was an aggregate of your other desires. We want more because we're meant to desire more.

Transgender people face a rudimentary desire even simpler than the abstract concepts of life, liberty, and the pursuit of happiness. We have one big desire to tackle before we get to those. Acceptance.

TRANSITIONING IS NOT THE END GOAL IN LIFE

I often joke to people that there isn't a block of time in my day dedicated to transitioning. That notion may seem pretty obvious on paper, but transitioning itself is often described as a tough and difficult journey. Things that are described in fashions similar to Frodo's quest to deliver the Ring to Mordor tend to sound time consuming.

Here's another "bombshell" for you. Transitioning isn't the only thing transgender people want in life. For many, myself included, it represents the beginning of a meta-phorically endless sea of opportunity. Like real oceans, the dream gets pretty polluted when you think of all the big-otry and other obstacles standing in the way of the LGBT community.

There's a derogatory metaphor that blames transgen-der people for the decline of America. "We used to want to put a man on the moon, now all we want is to put a man in the women's restroom." This is wrong for many reasons, but the one that interests me the most is the notion that as-pirations to literally reach for the stars somehow correlates to wanting to take a leak in peace in a smelly public facility.

The right to go to the bathroom is most certainly not the only thing transgender people want. That shouldn't even be a thing that people have to think about wanting, but it has to be because other people decided to try and take that basic right away. Who's really setting the bar low for the American dream?

This may come as a surprise to many, hopefully not, but transgender people want the same things everyone else wants. Careers, family, general prosperity. Transitioning is never the end goal, but rather, the means to make ev-erything else happen. We just want the same opportuni-ties as anyone else. To be judged on merit. Actual merit.

No discrimination. Is that too much to ask? We don't want "extra rights," just the same ones that everyone else is supposed to be afforded.

It is valuable to spell this basic stuff out for everyone. That transgender people are people with ambitions beyond prancing around in fancy new clothes. Reminds us all of what really matters. That we are human.

One final thing that transgender people want that everyone else also wants. Happiness. Everyone has a unique perspective regarding that concept, influenced by their own individual circumstances. Transgender people who held off on transitioning for fear of societal rejection try to live out a modified consolation prize version of happiness. Life does not work like that.

DEFINING "NATURAL"

A common insult levied against transgender people is that we aren't "natural." Natural in this instance being a pejorative used to denote the fact that many of us use hormones created in a lab or have surgery to change our appearances. Apparently, these are the standards for what constitutes a natural human existence.

Men use Viagra when their trouser snakes are having trouble springing to action. Women can use surrogates to have biological offspring if they face trouble with their own organs. The "natural" decision in either case might be to assume that nature does not want you to have offspring if your reproductive organs have problems, but such a mentality contradicts everything we know about human history.

Human beings don't really care what nature thinks. We build houses in places where it snows or floods a lot. We cure diseases that would otherwise kill millions, if not billions, of people. We wear Nike sneakers to protect our feet from the heat of asphalt, that we laid down because our cars didn't jive well with the terrain's previous layout. We can't fly on our own, so we made spaceships to travel to places where we can't even breathe the air.

Natural is a great word to read on a smoothie menu or to use as a hashtag for the picture of the sky from your morning hike. Elsewhere, not so much. We, as people, aren't too fond of "natural." When nature does something we don't like, we tend to figure out a way around it. That spirit that defines humanity, that is natural.

SOME BASIC QUESTIONS FOR THE CHURCH'S STANCE AGAINST THE LGBT COMMUNITY

The Church, referring to both the Catholic Church and others who adopt similar positions on LGBT issues, has a lot of problems with us queer folk. I have some questions I'd like to ask The Church. Maybe when we're done, we can get back to loving each other.

1. **Why would gay marriage threaten non-gay marriage?**

I don't know about you, but I don't know many gay people who want to be in a gay marriage with a person of the opposite sex. That whole idea kind of misses the point of being gay. Now, you might be wondering about the people who believe that marriage is an institution between one man and one woman, but that's not what we're talking about. Before we can get to that, we have to figure out this whole threatening business, because trans people are often treated as threats, for some reason. Maybe if The Church can figuratively sit down, or kneel, and think about this stuff for a while, it could either come up with a proper reason, or give up the fight entirely.

For gay marriage to be a threat to non-gay marriage, it has to have some sort of negative impact on the latter. For example, gay marriage could pose a threat to non-gay marriage if no priest were ever available to perform non-gay wedding ceremonies because they were all too busy presiding over gay weddings. This cannot be the case because many churches do not allow gay weddings, though many do allow gay priests, as long as they are not too public with their actions.

There is a threat posed in the sense that every gay marriage means that there are two fewer people on this earth who could engage in a non-gay marriage, presumably with alternative suitors. We tend to frown upon this idea nowadays. Other than that, I'm not seeing any threats. It's almost as if the idea of gay marriage being a threat was invented as an excuse because The Church simply doesn't like gay marriage.

You can roll your eyes at this logic all you want. Much

of it does feel like stating the obvious, but sometimes the obvious needs to be stated because the obvious is not always considered. The idea that gay marriage is a threat to any other kind of marriage is ridiculous, but also something that is floated around quite often, unchecked. It is easily debunked as a concept of pure stupidity, but that requires somebody to actually follow these trains of thought back to their origins. For many, it's easier and far more pleasant to not think about this stuff.

What does The Church's views on gay marriage have to do with transgender people? Pope Francis himself once referred to gender theory as "a great enemy of marriage,"[9] though he did not go into further detail. The Church sees us as a threat for some strange reason. Why? Who knows.

2. Why does marriage need to be between a man and a woman?

This argument against gay marriage centers around the meaning of a word. Marriage. According to this logic, used by politicians for many years, marriage is strictly between a man and a woman. Efforts to include same sex nuptials into this definition apparently cheapen the meaning of the word, for reasons that have never been fully explained. Advocates for this argument also often bring up the history of marriage as a religious ceremony, pointing to various institutions' opposition to gay marriage as further evidence for why it should not be allowed, despite the whole separation of church and state thing that we're supposed to care about.

The way that argument spells itself out should resemble a debate over the pronunciation of the word tomato. It never really looks that way, mostly because the meaning of a word is not really what's at stake. Marriage cannot just be a religious institution because there are legal implications of such a union.

Now, you may find some extremists who would argue that marriage strictly incorporates the ceremonial nature of the religious ritual, thereby excluding gay marriages from accurately fitting under the umbrella. That might make sense if people regularly had religious marriage ceremonies with no intention of ever actually obtaining a marriage license. Since this argument is over a word, it is important to note that the people who want marriage to strictly refer to a religious matter, never use it in a strictly religious function.

The battle for marriage equality still wages on, even after the outcome of *Obergefell v. Hodges* was celebrated throughout the land. It bears a lot of resemblance to the legitimacy debate that trans people face. People want to argue over the semantics of the words involved, ignoring that the fight is not about terminology. It is about what these words represent.

We all know the debate is not actually about words. If that were true, the majority of the people who argued that "marriage" was between a man and a woman would still support full equality for gay couples who engaged in their version of a margarine substitute. We know that's not how they really feel. The terminology war is as much as a sham as the legitimacy debate.

3. Isn't there an actual threat to marriage? What about that thing called divorce?

Roughly half of all marriages end in divorce. Many millennials aren't even bothering to get hitched at all. What is causing the decline of the immortal words, "'Til death do us part"?

I don't hear many people outright blaming gays for divorce, though there are those evangelical pastors who point to us as responsible for the erosion of Western society. This of course is nothing but a dog-whistle intended to send the message that immigrants and the LGBT community are really to blame for all problems everywhere.

Divorce is neither a good thing nor a bad thing. It is in fact, a threat to marriage, in the sense that divorce is only one of two ways a marriage can end. The other, death, is not something humans have been able to tackle despite centuries of progress. The concept of an annulment exists separately to protect marriage, functioning not as the end of a union, but as a way to pretend it never even happened. Being a threat to marriage cannot itself be bad, for marriage itself is neither good nor bad. There are good marriages and there are bad marriages. The institution might be a religious sacrament, but is it really something that should be propped up at all costs? Is it worth ruining someone's life over? Apparently, The Church thinks so.

The argument could be made that marriage isn't taken as seriously as it used to be, with couples who throw in the towel months after making their vows. Fine, but that has nothing to do with LGBT people. Pretending otherwise is just hateful.

4. Why is The Church so obsessed with sex?

One excuse against gay marriage centers around the idea that marriage, and by extension, sex, exists primarily as a vessel for procreation. This idea is complicated by The Church's fairly non-controversial stance allowing couples who cannot naturally conceive to marry and subsequently express their love through intercourse. A rule excluding sterile men and barren women would be cruel, and fairly ridiculous considering that setback doesn't mean the couple wouldn't be able to raise a family. There are, in fact, other ways.

Gay couples can raise families too, whether through adoption or surrogates, despite The Church's best efforts. This is a beautiful thing for lots of different reasons, chief among them that there are a lot of orphan kids out there who actually need loving homes. The Church should focus its efforts more on those kids who need help rather than the abstract future children that they believe should only be raised by heterosexual couples.

Furthermore, we should also acknowledge that not every person wants to be a parent, or is fit to be one. That's okay. Certainly better than the idea that everyone should procreate, which is much closer to The Church's position than the reverse. The earth has a lot of people. It doesn't "need" anymore, mostly because the human race is highly unlikely to ever face extinction for a lack of reproduction. Nuclear war is at least 92% more likely to be the cause of the grand finale.

We shouldn't shame people who don't want to have

kids, or couples that want to be loving parents. Their intentions should be what matters, not arbitrary rules. You don't hear of many people who have to deal with childhood trauma caused by their parents' love. The absence of that vital affection is the real danger. Maybe The Church should worry more about that instead of focusing all its efforts on sex. It's pretty weird, even before you consider The Church's various sex scandals over the past few decades.

5. What would Jesus think of transgender people?

The biblical Jesus was a pretty chill revolutionary who liked hanging out with people that polite society wasn't too fond of. I imagine that there would be no fewer than three transgender apostles if He were to come back today. We are certainly less controversial than tax collectors were back then. Possibly, just maybe, even the lepers too!

The Church's positions on the LGBT community contradict everything we're taught about this peace-loving hippie who walked the earth two thousand years ago. Where is all that stuff in the New Testament about the people He wants us to hate? Which gospel can we find "love thy neighbor, unless they are gay" located?

Now some can argue that The Church loves LGBT people, as long as we stay chaste for life and never find any happiness of our own that The Church says comes from heterosexual marriage. This is nonsense. It's kind of like inviting someone over for dinner but telling them they have to eat instant ramen noodles instead of the prime rib you've prepared for yourself and the rest of your guests.

Would you really want to go to the dinner, even if the ramen happened to be your favorite flavor?

If Jesus loves everyone, He loves transgender people too. If we're to believe that He loves us all unconditionally, that would suggest that He doesn't only want some of us to be happy. There are no secret conditions. If that isn't true, that He only wants straight people to be happy, maybe we should stop giving Him an hour of our Sunday every weekend. Many of us already have. I wonder why…

DO WE KNOW WHAT LOVE IS?

Pose this question to the birther: Why do humans love the ones they love? Birthers like to focus on biology and the "natural order of things" without really understanding that human beings are different from animals. That distinction used to be noted by the fact that humans mate for life, unlike most species, save for a few such as swans, coyotes, and beavers. Seems kind of weird nowadays with the divorce rate being what it is.

So what is love, beyond the song from *A Night at the Roxbury*? Plenty of self-help books have tried to explain the sensation, but it would be wrong to say we have anything even resembling a consensus opinion on the matter. We can see love, when two people show that unmistakable affection for each other, but we cannot explain how it got there, even with a map. While the subject of romance certainly keeps a lot of people up at night, we as a society have plugged along just fine without any clear answers for why anyone feels this strange emotion.

Love is real. Love is completely illogical. Love is definitely not biological. Humans do not spontaneously find themselves unable to function until they've gotten the love out of their system. Our reproductive instincts aren't that primitive. We have a term for the people who can't control their urges to act in spite of the lack of consent. We put those kinds of people in jail.

We're okay not knowing what love is. We love the feeling anyway. That completely illogical emotion feels really good. Logic does not need to play a role.

FEELINGS ARE NOT AUTOMATICALLY WORTH LESS THAN SCIENCE

Science is not perfect. It is not always factual. Scientists used to believe the world was flat. Aristotle, widely accepted as one of the greatest philosophical minds of all time, believed that rocks fell to the ground because that was where they were supposed to be. Not because of that thing called gravity. We do not know if our cats really want to kill us.

What exactly is the scientific consensus on transgender people that the birthers like to abstractly cite in their attacks? Does it say that your gender identity is defined at birth somewhere in the "Book of Science"? This is a serious question, that should have an easy answer given how often science is deployed to settle this matter.

Putting facts and feelings into two separate categories makes sense for a number of reasons, many of them legitimate. Inevitably, one of those reasons is that it feels good. The idea of scientific fact is comforting as it creates a sense of order, impenetrable logic that can comfort the mind in times of uncertainty. Unfortunately, there's just so much out there we don't know, like what was up with the *Lost* finale. Some things are best left unexplored.

Feelings get a bad rap. It is true that feelings can cause the mind to act irrationally in times of anger or hunger, (creating the wonderful term "hangry") or other emotions. However, there are times when feelings guide us in the right direction.

Think about a stomachache. How do you know you have one? You feel it. You don't wave your iPhone up and down your stomach until Siri lets you know what's up. If it hurts enough, you go to a doctor. Oddly enough, the medical diagnosis does not involve any iPhone waving either, or any devices that look like something out of an episode of *Star Trek*.

The doctor can prescribe medicine that will cure the stomachache without having to cut you open for visual confirmation. You don't even need to take a test that can prove you have a stomachache. Imagine that! You can feel something *and* have that feeling inspected, diagnosed, and treated even though you'll never have absolute certainty that it was ever truly there.

Evidence is absolutely not absolute. It is not something we always care about, always. Sometimes feelings are enough. In the absence of an official "transgender test," that could provide us with irrefutable proof, feelings, coupled with therapy, just might be the better indicator.

Science, through medicine, has its role to play. Medical doctors administer HRT, using blood samples to monitor hormone doses among other things. Science is great, but sometimes, so are feelings.

The realms of faith, love, and identity care little for facts. The human experience cannot be summarized with a series of objective truths, which might be a good thing. If history tells us anything, it's that humanity has been wrong about a lot of stuff over the years.

WHAT IS THE TYPICAL MAN OR WOMAN?

Think about that question. It is simultaneously confusing, unanswerable, and important. Any image of any person immediately contradicts the idea of "typical," for whatever being you imagine has a skin color. Your image inevitably contains features that cannot represent any sizable majority of any demographic. We tend to call attempts to do so, stereotyping. Not good.

Does a cismale Oklahoman farmer share more in common with a transmale Oregonian farmer or a cismale Japanese farmer? Geography and biological sex organs are the sole known variables. The precise definition of "more" should not be important if there are universal ties that bind that link biological men together.

You may struggle with this answer without additional information, for good reason. Or you might pick the two

American farmers because while we don't know much about them other than that they live in the same country, it is safer to assume that they speak the same language than it is to assume the Oklahoman farmer is fluent in Japanese.

But if the Oklahoman and the Oregonian share more in common, how universal could the bonds that tie people together by their private parts really be? Private parts are the important distinction here since testosterone and estrogen can be manufactured without testicles and ovaries. If men are men and women are women and there's nothing transgender people can do to change that, why would culture matter? Universal traits are supposed to be, universal.

The idea of the typical man or woman is an interesting abstract concept. That's all it is. It works because people can substitute themselves in for the idea of "typical," providing a material example to contrast with transgender people, despite the obvious limitations. Using yourself as the example allows people to feel comfortable enough not to worry. No attempt to materialize that image would result in anything that fully embodied the true definition of "typical." That's the point. There is no universal man or woman, nor do people share some intricate bond because of the private parts they were born with.

Concepts of brotherhoods and sisterhoods are nice because they create community. Humans like to feel a part of something, which is part of the reason why it hurts when transgender people are excluded just because of a few differences that don't really tell us much at all. If those reasons do tell us something, someone should be able to offer a reason for why the Oregonian farmer shares more in common with the Japanese farmer based on something other than private parts. Those don't tell us much.

WHAT IS THE TRUE MEASURE OF A PERSON?

We claim to judge people by character. Centuries of studies on racial and gender inequality prove this to be largely a load of nonsense, but there are also other indicators. The "halo effect" points to attractiveness as a major indicator of success. There are even studies that suggest that taller people make more money.

Of course character matters. Just not very much, in comparison to a number of things that should not really matter, except for the fact that they do. We tell ourselves this because we can change our character, unlike our height or basic general features. It is in our control.

Transgender people have made a decision to be judged on a more authentic scale than we would be otherwise, if we stayed in the closet. Birthers point to the aesthetics through which people are judged: looks, clothes, etc. to suggest we're trying to be something we're not. In doing so, they forego the idea that character matters, in favor of the superficial nonsense. We as a nation should not really be okay with that kind of rationale.

TO THE "WOMYN-BORN WOMYN" MOVEMENT

Fuck off. Your exclusionary bullshit serves no purpose other than to create a breeding ground for unnecessary hate.

People are correct to note the difference in lived experience between transwomen and women who received that designation at birth. These are two distinct identities. We should not deny that simple truth.

It should not be used as a discriminatory tactic, which is what the Michigan Womyn's Music Festival did for years. It excluded us because of our birth genitals, which is dangerous, because a lot of other groups discriminate against us for the exact same reason.

The counterargument often presented by these "womyn-born womyn," also known as "trans-exclusionary radical feminists" (TERFs), presents a legitimate question. If there are two distinct identities, why can't one have its own event? The answer is simpler than you'd think.

Women's festivals were designed to celebrate the historically marginalized gender. Transgender women did not commit the marginalizing. There are those who might try to argue that transwomen have experienced "male privilege" and they're right. We've been on the receiving end of its negative effects. If they want to argue that we, meaning transwomen, were once the oppressors, well, I guess it needs to be said again. Fuck off. This nonsense is just another cog in the legitimacy debate.

It's not just me saying it. There is no more Michigan Womyn's Music Festival, which never managed to shake the controversy of its transgender discrimination. Women who fit the parameters of "womyn born womyn" hate that bullshit too. Enough is enough. We're not your enemies. Stop being ours.

RESIST THE URGE TO CLOSE YOURSELF OFF

I see events advertised as "closed off" for people who don't belong to the LGBT community, excluding the allies who support our cause. The term "safe space" floats around. While I understand that these decisions are made in the interest of protecting marginalized members of our society, seeing those kinds of disclaimers still makes me sad.

There aren't enough of us to win the fight for equality on our own. We need allies. Maybe those allies will understand when you don't want them at your functions, but they also might feel disengaged out of a sense of rejection. I wouldn't blame them. Plenty of people are homophobic, transphobic, or just generally bigoted. We shouldn't let this fact distract us from how many more are not.

Open yourself to the world. It is a scary notion that often flies in the face of logic, but a liberating one. We've been rejected long enough. We don't need a turn as the rejecters.

WHAT DO WE WANT? EQUALITY (THE REAL KIND)

Why is this so hard? We are taught in kindergarten to share and to be nice to each other. Everyone gets a turn on the swings, a cupcake in class, even if you aren't friends with the birthday girl/boy/person.

Those lessons are relatively useless. I do not say that lightly. The truth is, morality does not get you very far in most professions. Lawyers, hedge fund managers, and politicians have no need for right or wrong. It rarely factors into the equation, certainly not when anyone is actually caught doing something naughty.

We are okay with that. Like it? Maybe not, but that does not mean we care enough to actually do something about it. There is always some mechanism in place to prevent the status quo from changing, an ever-present barrier that makes you want to give up and go watch some Hulu Plus. We forget these lessons presented on *Sesame Street* somewhere along the way. That first moment you realized you could do something bad and get away with it, the truth becomes a deterrent, an obstacle that can be avoided if one can construct an alternate reality.

Equality is an abstract notion people do not care to consider, not when the alternative is far too convenient. It is easy not to care when you have no stakes in the game. We can make laws that say men and women must be treated equally and that you cannot discriminate against someone based on their sexual preferences or gender identity, but who is to enforce these rules on a daily basis across the country? Only we the people, flawed as we are.

ON THE SUBJECT OF GENDER FLUIDITY

Gender is a spectrum. Expressing oneself can include crossing over past the accepted boundaries of the traditional boy/girl binary. This is nothing new. Terms such as "tomboy" or "sissy" serve as derogatory identifiers attached to people who dared to push past what is "accepted" by polite society.

The label "gender fluid" itself represents a rejection of labels. Boy is a label. Girl is a label. Fluidity between the two acknowledges the artificial limits of these social constructs, for the people who dare to venture back and forth do so with the understanding that there are those who will seek to punish this nonconformity.

Gender fluid does not necessarily indicate an absence of gender either. One who is right handed does not go through life never utilizing their south paw. People try to dismiss this as a "fad," or a phase in someone's life. Maybe it is. Or maybe it wasn't and the social stigma merely forced the person to alter course. We can't know for sure. Best to let people figure life out on their own terms.

SEXUALITY IS MORE FLUID THAN YOU THINK

There is nothing stopping a gay man from having sex with a woman. You might think this would make the gay person straight, but we tend to determine sexuality by attraction, not by the act of sex itself. A gay person can physically have sex with a member of the opposite sex and still be gay. It is possible. The vagina does not cause the penis to go limp like a magnet repelling a similar pole. This pole could, in theory, work.

Sexuality as we perceive it exists in relation to the gender binary. We recognize the concept of attractive members of our own sex, even if we think we're only attracted to those belonging to the opposite. If you are a man, recognizing a fellow attractive man is not the same as wanting to have sex with that man, but attraction also doesn't work like that. There are steps involved, including the whole "courting" process in between. Attraction is really only the mechanism that sets everything else in motion. There's a reason people don't walk up to people they find attractive at bars and immediately ask, "Would you like to have sex with me?" The world doesn't work like that.

A straight man could be courted by a gay man and end up falling in love. Believe it or not, it has happened. The fact that it doesn't happen very often, or that we don't really talk about that kind of stuff, reflects more on society's view of the binary than anything else.

This is not meant to suggest that everyone is bisexual, but we all could be. It isn't something we tend to think about unless we have those attractions. You could say that not having those attractions indicates that one is not gay or bisexual, but this is an oversimplification. Gay or straight is not the typical either/or scenario. Straight people haven't faced countless acts of oppression and discrimination over the course of recorded history for being straight. The binary may offer a choice, but it's certainly a loaded one. There's always been a lot of pressure to feel a certain way sexually.

Sexuality is a tricky concept that certainly allows for plenty of wiggle room beyond the gay/straight option. It didn't used to, which is why we are where we are. There are plenty of reasons why this should change.

ANAL SEX FEELS GOOD, GUYS (IT'S OKAY TO ADMIT IT)

The taboo sends shivers down your spine. You're not supposed to like putting things up there, according to many interpretations of the good book. It's even a crime in many countries.

A shame. Feels great. The prostate loves its stimulation. Those magazines offering tips on how to improve your sex life weren't joking about that. See for yourself!

What do parents say when kids express concern over new food on their plates? Don't knock something until you try it. Plenty of people refuse to try anal sex. Is it because they know they won't like it? It can't be, because they didn't try it.

Their refusal might be because they are worried it might make them gay, or suggest to others that they are. These are silly concerns. A fear of being gay has never stopped someone from being gay. Despite the inclinations of some men to boast about their sexual prowess, you don't actually have to talk about what goes on behind closed doors. Why worry about something that feels good and doesn't hurt anyone?

There is even a special term for when women don a strap-on to perform the deed. Pegging. The male ego doesn't love the term anal sex, so a euphemism was created. The pleasure is still the same, no matter the terminology. Pegging is a silly term. Here's a better one: anal sex. The shivers return, as the fragile ego seeks its shelter.

The world would be a better place if all men experienced anal sex at least once in their lives, whether from a woman or a man. Society might even stop pretending that LGBT people suffer from some weird perversion. If God created all of us, He also created those fun pleasure spots up there. Why wouldn't He want you to enjoy them?

THE ATTRACTION PARADOX

Some people say that those who refuse to date transgender people are bigots. I hate to assign broad labels to people, especially in the complex murky waters of love, but it has to be fundamentally true. It is certainly no different from saying you wouldn't date a member of a minority group.

The counterargument to this charge often revolves around the idea that transgender people cannot have children, which is not accurate. Many people, myself included, have taken measures to preserve our ability to reproduce before transitioning. A more accurate charge to levy would be that I cannot impregnate a woman through penetrative sex and cannot be impregnated through penetrative sex with a man.

It is true that this distinction may do little to change some people's minds. "The heart wants what it wants," is an age old term to explain the bizarre laws of attraction. I can't explain what makes people attracted to other people. I can tell you one thing that doesn't really matter, even if it seems like it should.

Fertility.

You may feel a natural urge to disagree with this idea. How many people take fertility tests before marriage? How often has that topic even come up with anyone you've dated casually? The prospect of kids is something that inevitably comes up, but we don't hear of many first dates where the subject of swimmer mobility or how many eggs a woman has left comes up. It's weird to think about. The prospect of having to use in vitro fertilization or other methods is generally not considered a deal breaker anymore.

But apparently, this whole subject is still really, really important. Not necessarily important enough to ask about before marriage, but a big enough deal that a person can decide they don't want to date trans people while also being uncomfortable with the idea that such a sentiment might make one a bigot.

It must be one or the other.

People are uncomfortable with being called bigots for not wanting to date trans people because we as a society are not really all that comfortable with trans people in general. Americans are having fewer children. Articles on why millennials aren't having kids litter the internet. It is not the real reason people won't date transgender people. The reason is actually simpler in many ways, though more complex in others. We're marginalized, fetishized, castigated as freaks. Too often we're denied the chance to even be viewed as human, let alone attractive.

Think of the prospects of your high school's head cheerleader ever dating the biggest nerd in your class. That notion is ridiculous because it seems unlikely to ever happen, even though plenty of science-oriented children grow up to marry conventionally attractive partners. It has nothing to do with the magnetic poles being off, repelling the cheerleader from the nerd. Only that the social construct of high school does not permit anyone to seriously entertain this notion. It is not considered.

The real world functions like high school in some ways. There's the overbearing boss who can often resemble a schoolyard bully. There's the attractive person at the bar that you could never possibly see yourself talking to unless some cosmic factors intervened on your behalf, like being bitten by a radioactive spider. Unlike high school, hopefully more people in your general orbit, perhaps yourself included, are aware that these are arbitrary societal constructs that are not necessarily "real," even if true in isolated examples.

"BUT, I'M JUST NOT ATTRACTED TO TRANSGENDER PEOPLE"

What does this mean? For a statement like that to be considered anything other than bigoted, transgender people would have to fit some kind of generalized mold. There may be an image in your head of someone with big breasts and a penis that you saw on a porn site. Or an image of Caitlyn Jenner. It is not that important. All that really matters is that you understand that this singular image cannot accurately represent a full group of people. It is kind of a problem if you don't.

There is some murky water here. If you are a straight person who is really obsessed with your heterosexuality, you may not love the idea of pre-op transwomen because of the whole penis situation. To be perfectly honest, I'm not a huge fan of mine either. This is not however, a valid justification for why someone would not be attracted to transgender people. Chiefly because not all transgender people have penises.

Physical attraction is only one element of what goes into finding a partner. We as a society are trained to laugh at the people who say they are attracted to someone for their personality, but it is a valid consideration. You don't hear of many happy marriages built solely on carnal attraction.

Try imagining what the mold of the transgender personality might look like. Anything? Bueller? Bueller?

Didn't think so.

Attraction itself in all its forms is only one part of this grand equation. Proximity and luck are also major factors, perhaps even more so. The notion of "the one" is a cute idea backed by pretty much every romance story ever crafted. The real world is far more practical.

THE FANTASTICAL PORN ILLUSION

The porn industry employs a lot of transgender people. Porn featuring transgender actors is extremely popular. In a world where transgender people are discriminated against at work, often legally, this industry, that people do not necessarily enjoy discussing in mixed company, offers work to people who need it. However you feel about that does not really alter the aesthetics of reality.

The fact that people do not like talking about porn does not mean that people are not watching porn. A lot of those people are watching transgender porn, hearing phrases like "t-girl," "she-male," and "chick with a dick," alongside the increasingly controversial term "transsexual," which is at least still used scientifically. What are we supposed to think will happen if a group's sole form of representation comes from portrayals by adult film actors on websites with much larger streaming fees than Netflix?

Many people's sole exposure to transgender people is through porn. No one wants to admit that because it would mean that we admitted that people actually watch porn. There is however, a lot of porn on the internet. Some might even consider it the internet's true calling.

There are frequent controversies over typecasting in Hollywood, for good reason. People don't want society turning back the clock because of a character in a hit movie, even if we accept the fact that one character in one film cannot be expected to represent an entire minority subgroup. We're still afraid it might.

There are countless studies on the negative effects of porn on the brain. Imagine what would happen if we took the negative effects of stereotyping combined with the worst ramifications of habitual porn viewing on societal interactions and amplified that with the scarcity of transgender people in every day life. Not good!

Imagine if you met a Klingon from *Star Trek*. After getting over the initial shock that a species from a popular multimedia franchise was real, you'd probably have some basic assumptions if you were familiar with the series. You may think they were aggressive, thirsty for bloodwine. This Klingon could be a pacifist teetotaler, who does not even believe in Sto-vo-kor. The conventional stereotype would be wrong.

You may be wondering why a fictional species was used in this example instead a real life minority group. It is important to remember that again, there are not many transgender people in the world. A person's view of African Americans might be unfairly jaded by stereotypes on TV, but it is safe to say that a majority of Americans have actually interacted with a black person. The same cannot be said for transgender people, especially when our very legitimacy is still called into question. To the people who only know transgender people through characters played in pornographic films, we are the fiction they see on their screens at home, often while hiding from their parents/ spouses, tissue or sock in hand.

None of this is meant to disparage the porn industry, or the people who enjoy it. It should go without saying that porn does not mirror reality, but maybe it is worth saying again. Porn does not mirror reality. Generalizations can be dangerous, but it is safe to say that the transgender community as a whole more closely resembles the general public than their pornographic counterparts. Duh.

LET US HAVE OUR CHANCE AT LOVE

Saying that people who refuse to date trans people are bigots might be accurate, but it is also largely irrelevant. Those words won't cause anyone to feel attraction to a group they were previously repulsed by. Fortunately, that's not really necessary.

People are allowed to not be attracted to full minority groups. That opinion is generally not allowed to be uttered out loud in polite society. That is the kind of statement that would get somebody into a lot of trouble, and for good reasons. Chief among them being that it is a horrible thing to say. It should not be okay to say about transgender people, even if you agree with the sentiment.

No one should have any illusions that we'll live in a world where transgender people face no additional societal hardships due to our gender identity any time soon.

Probably not in my lifetime. Love is an idea clouded by countless fictional portrayals of what it means. In reality, it's far more practical. People who spend a lot of time around certain people are bound to develop certain feelings. Time is a much more powerful force than fate.

That requires a base level of attraction that comes from somewhere deep inside each individual. The castigation and marginalization of transgender people interferes with our ability to even be considered as potential suitors, something that minority groups face in every culture. We are not freaks, but the label itself causes plenty of damage in a world where society's influence leads our minds down paths we aren't even fully aware of.

There are people who are attracted to transgender people, both for our beautiful looks and our lovely personalities. We date. We get married and live happy lives. The birthers may find this hard to believe because they aren't attracted to us, but that's okay. No one's asking them to be.

Just like everyone else, we all want our chance at love. That chance should not be impeded by socially acceptable bigotry. Bigotry shouldn't be socially acceptable, even if it's what you feel deep down inside. Much of this book argues for many kinds of liberation. Bigoted thoughts should stay repressed.

CAN ANYONE BE TRANSGENDER?

This is a favorite talking point for the people on the right. According to this logic, one of the big reasons why transgender people should not have rights is that it could lead to people claiming false status as trans, to reap some sort of benefit. The two most common examples of these so-called advantages are that people could pretend to be transgender in order to play on a sports team or to use the bathroom designated for the opposite sex. Generally, these examples point the finger at transgender women.

There are many, many things wrong with this concept. Chief among them being the idea that anyone would undergo such an arduous process, permanently changing their bodies, for seemingly brief gains. Again, I point to bathrooms as they exist in reality, as smelly places where people avoid touching the floor for any reason, let alone to peep into another stall. Not the carnival of fun theoretical version that gets tossed around.

Let's create an example to look at how a person might try to get a leg up in sports by pretending to be transgender. Suppose there's this fairly good soccer player in high school. Varsity boys' team. On the cusp of starting. Giving this person an age is problematic. If this person is a freshman or a sophomore, one would think that waiting a year or two might be a smarter plan. Senior year is obviously a bit too late. Junior year is really the only one that could fit as a time in someone's life where they might look to changing their gender solely for the chance to start on a high school sports team. It is crucial that this example is mildly realistic, because the birthers rarely seem to care about reality.

In case you forgot, it is also important to remember that there are other ways to become a star athlete besides changing your gender. Something called hard work or effort or determination. Hard work might sound hard, but no sane person would ever call transitioning easy. Though right now, we have to put aside what a sane person might think of this plan as well.

So this student really wants to get recruited for college, and thinks that becoming a woman is the only way to achieve that goal. For many who don't know really know how transitioning works, the logical next step might appear to be snap your fingers and receive your girls' uniform in time for the big game. But that's not how this would work if someone ever actually tried this con.

This person would have to somehow convince their parents that this wasn't a ruse thought up on a whim, followed by at least a few months of counseling. Maybe this person would be able to start HRT after a few months or so, but that's entirely contingent on finding a doctor who not only specializes in transgender patients, but is also willing to administer life-altering hormones to a minor. That alone would rule out a large chunk of the country, and the process of starting hormones tends to take a while unless you found a good doctor who isn't booked for months on the first try.

This isn't the final step either if the kid manages to get this far. There's also the question of whether or not the school would actually let him, now her, play. Given that college recruitment is the end goal, following the NCAA guidelines seems to make sense. Except the NCAA requires MTF transgender students to be on testosterone suppressants for a year. The timeline would certainly be cutting it close if this person wanted to take the field for the girls' team in time for senior year, assuming no parents in the school district put up a fight like the one Gavin Grimm faces, just for wanting to use his proper bathroom.

Now, you might point out that I didn't necessarily describe the best case scenario. It is possible a school board would be fully accommodating and willing to waive any kind of regulation. A scout would almost assuredly still want a detailed medical report before offering any letters of intent. In theory, this *could* work. It would rely on both a seamless performance by the athlete, who would need to be fully rational while making a completely irrational decision, as well as little to no resistance from the outside community.

I wouldn't be concerned with the best case scenario either, since transgender people always face resistance in life. The odds of whether or not it would work are far more important to a person actually considering this plan. One would think, given everything that could go wrong and the whole issue of living the rest of your life as a member of a gender you don't actually align with, that this was not a good idea.

You might think this example is stupid and a big waste of time. Problem is, people do try to make this argument. You hear it on Fox News whenever a story about a trans athlete pops up. What they fail to realize is that this isn't a fun process. No one wants to be subjected to national scrutiny because a school board didn't want to let them play a game.

To answer the hypothetical offered by right wing

grandstanders, I actually would support the right of a person who went through that process to be allowed to play, even if their intentions were suspect. I don't think it's ever actually happened in this country for many reasons, including ones mentioned in this section, but I believe that anyone who meets the accepted reasonable criteria should not have their motives questioned by anyone who couldn't possibly know what it feels like to be in their shoes. Or their soccer cleats.

WHAT ABOUT THE ACTUAL PRETENDERS?

This is a confusing subject. When someone you know tells you they are "gender fluid" without really going into specifics as to how this proclamation has affected their life in any way, the mind can turn to the question, "How can this be?" as if you are being fed a load of nonsense.

Which you very well might be. There is no legitimacy test. A person telling you they are "gender fluid," or something of the sort, may in fact, not be. It could all be an experiment and this person may not identify as gender fluid later on in life, even perhaps a week later. You have no real way of knowing, reflective of the fact that someone else's identity really isn't any of your business.

There is the perception that this kind of uncertainty is damaging to the transgender community at large. The idea that someone could claim to belong to that category on a whim, before quickly abandoning the label in favor of a new trend, a new identity, hurts the public perception of the rest of us who have to fight for our legitimacy in the absence of an actual test. This can happen when people try to "find" themselves. It is okay. Introspection is usually a good thing. There isn't really supposed to be a right or a wrong answer for the bigger picture types of questions, which is for the best when you think about it. Gatekeeping is an ugly practice. People have a right to figure out themselves on their own terms, regardless of any outcome. The general public isn't owed an explanation for a person's identity, however much they may not understand it.

Following that train of thought might lead one to dismiss trans people outright, as if the idea of one uncertain soul in our midst invalidates us all. That notion is fairly ridiculous. An individual's choices do not reflect those of an entire community under any circumstances. Furthermore, it forces a revealing spotlight on the idea of policing transgender people's identities at all.

There can be no broad "transgender" litmus test because the idea of establishing any set of criteria is extremely problematic. Hormones? Sex reassignment surgery? Birth certificate gender change? Name change? These are all aspects of the transgender experience, but few would argue that your gender identity would be rendered inauthentic because you did not appear before a judge in your birth state to have a piece of paper altered. Something can't be a qualifier if its disqualification changes nothing.

Beyond that, it is fairly easy to tell the difference between a college student who has publicly changed their gender identity five times in a single semester and a transgender person who lives as a member of the gender opposite from their designated sex. The college student is not doing anything wrong either. The idea that such experimentation with the rules of gender reflects in any way, shape, or form back on the transgender community as a whole is preposterous, an idea propagated by the birthers as a way to continue fighting the legitimacy debate.

Why does the public need to know the specific details of someone's identity? Does it really matter? To some people that answer is yes, but they never seem to want to explain why.

ON THE NUMBER OF GENDERS

There are a lot of memes mocking the idea that there are more than two genders. Society likes memes. They can be very funny, but they also make it easy to not have to think about something. Not a lot of words involved in your average meme.

How strange is it? We already have a spectrum, from the lipstick femme to the butch. While these terms do not note additional genders, they do represent the fluid nature of how we view the boy/girl binary, which only officially acknowledges two options. Clearly there is some wiggle room for additional categories.

We already have androgyny. Is agender really that much more of a stretch? If we have the absence of gender and a fairly fluid interpretation of the binary that encompasses the full range of both its options, infinite genders really represents a slightly different way of recognizing the much more tangible concept of endless possibilities.

It is hard to see why this is a big deal, or why it affects the general population in any substantive way. If someone says they are agender, bigender, polygender, or genderfluid, does that really have a negative impact on your life? If it does, who does that fact really reflect back on?

THE BATHROOM CHRONICLES

The birthers love talking about the concept of "transgender bathrooms." This term is effective in the sense that it suggests that we transgender people are the ones advocating for a cosmic shift in accepted bathroom protocol, conveniently forgetting that before these bathroom bills, men, women, and everyone in between did their business in peace and harmony. The birthers are the ones who want a new world order, governing over washrooms across the land, not transgender people.

As if this book did not contain enough talk of toilets already, here is a ten-part saga through the various issues presented by the birthers' "solutions" to the problems that they want us to believe actually exist.

Part One: The Urinal Predicament

The only portion of the transgender population who are in a position to use a urinal are transmen who have undergone bottom surgery. This is only an important detail because the urinal represents the sole area of a public bathroom where people would possibly be in a position to have their junk out for someone else to see. Typically, people don't walk around bathrooms with their pants down.

As anyone who's used a urinal can attest, it's pretty easy to use one without having to see anyone else's genitalia. You pretty much have to go out of your way to see a penis that is not your own. By going out of your way, I mean you'd have to quite obviously sneak a peek, with little sneaking involved, since urinals are not protected by stall doors. Some don't even have barriers between them. Anyone waiting in line would see if you were trying to do anything other than pee while standing at a urinal. Given that they presumably need to use one, I doubt they'd be too happy to see someone fooling around, holding up the line.

Birthers often point to the potential difference in genitalia as a reason to ban transgender people from bathrooms and locker rooms. People have not been allowed to swim naked in public pools for decades, though the fact that they ever were casts doubt as to the potential risks involved with the human eye coming into contact with someone else's reproductive appendage. Bathrooms and locker rooms hardly resemble nudist colonies.

It is unclear what correlation there is between urinals and a potential danger posed by the extremely small portion of the transgender population who would use them. You would think there would be, if these laws are supposed to have any practical value. Did any of these congressman ever ask if urinals were dangerous before they cast their vote? I doubt it.

Part Two: The Magical Funhouse Peepshow Paradox

Since when were bathrooms these places where wild sexual deviations and orgies occurred on even a semi-recurring basis? I've been in a lot of public bathrooms and have never witnessed or overheard any sexual acts being performed. I've never had someone stick their head under my stall in hopes of obtaining a view of my private parts. I've never seen anyone try to do anything like that. I don't know anyone who has.

This may not surprise you. It should, in theory, surprise someone. The lack of police reports on rising bathroom sex seems to suggest that all this coitus isn't happening. Despite this, we have these new bathroom laws designed to "protect" people. From what exactly?

No sex, consensual or otherwise, is allowed in public bathrooms, just as sex is not allowed in public. The whole notion of public displays of affection, or PDAs, is frowned upon by a large section of the population and that's just kissing. No one wants to see the rest of the show.

These bathroom bills also suggest that these public facilities are great places to catch a glimpse of someone else's private parts. This logic completely ignores the extremely limited viewing angles into a public stall. There are really only two ways, and neither really offers any protection from getting caught.

The first involves staring through that small little space between the door and the edge of the stall. This requires the viewer to squint, offering a very limited angle of what's actually inside. It would be very obvious to anyone else in the bathroom, including the person in the stall, that there was a peeper in their midst.

The second method requires the person to physically get down on the dirty bathroom floor to stick their head under the stall for a shot at seeing someone else's genitals, an image which could be easily obstructed by the person's clothes, or the angle of their knees. There are numerous problems with this scenario. Perhaps the biggest issue is that this strategy also ensures that the person will be caught in the middle of the act of peeping. The question of desired outcome for such a gamble must be considered. What would a person really hope to gain by sticking their head under a bathroom stall, besides a place on their state's sex offender registry?

It seems as though public bathrooms already have built-in mechanisms against these kinds of intrusions. They're called stalls. One can try to get around them at their own inevitable peril.

Part Three: The Deviance Dilemma

No one really wants to say this out loud, but the bathroom bill is crafted under the pretense that transgender people are sexual deviants. There are no credible studies that support this concept. Such logic seems more likely to be centered around the hetero-masculine notion that every person born with a penis must want to use it at all times.

Why does the public need to be "protected" from transgender people? This question is not asked often enough. We are different, that is true. There is no direct correlation between being different and being dangerous, despite what white supremacy groups might try to tell you.

There is plenty of logic to suggest that transgender people are actually less likely to be sexual deviants. A potential side effect of HRT is a decreased libido, which is only natural when the testicles encounter pills described as "testosterone blockers." I don't know about you, but I would tend to think that people who seek sex in a public bathroom would have a higher sex drive than normal, not lower. Generalities are tricky.

Children often invent a fictional disease carried by members of the opposite sex. Remember cooties? There wasn't much of a scientific process that went into diagnosing cooties. If you were a boy and you saw a girl, that was often enough evidence to suggest that this girl might have cooties.

The suggestion that transgender people are somehow linked to bathroom debauchery, in the absence of any data backing such a correlation, is no different. The only difference is that adults aren't in kindergarten anymore. Yet the nonsense continues.

Part Four: The Pretender Pickle

This is an argument that birthers love to make. Apparently, if you are going to let transgender people use the bathroom they feel most comfortable in, this will lead to people changing their gender on a whim in order to use whatever bathroom they like. This logic is once again built on the false idea that being transgender is a choice.

Comfort is something discussed in relation to transgender issues quite a lot. People who do not necessarily understand the transgender identity often offer variations of "whatever they're comfortable with," or "whatever makes them happy." I don't know about you, but the idea of wearing clothes typically designated for one gender and walking into a bathroom typically designated for people of the opposite sex does not appear to lead to many happy outcomes. It seems like a great way to get yelled at by a lot of people. This is what the birthers want for us.

The birthers subtly try to suggest that men will pretend to be transgender to use the women's bathroom, ignoring that society itself lacks a kind of formal process denoting the change from one gender to another. A person presenting as male will still be seen as male by everyone else even if they announced publicly "I am now transgender," for everyone in their general vicinity to hear. A man dressed as a man who walks into the women's bathroom could in theory walk in and out without running into conflict. Birthers like to believe that there is this possibility that if the man was caught by a woman upset with his presence in the bathroom, he could somehow evade taking responsibility by claiming "transgender status."

We've already covered the numerous issues presented by trying to actually catch a glimpse of other people's private parts as well as how problematic it is to "pretend" being transgender. This potential scenario presented by the birthers is ridiculous. Even if it wasn't, it still isn't a very good reason to strip an entire minority group of our basic human rights.

Bad behavior never excuses more bad behavior. Especially when the first act is a theoretical example that doesn't actually happen and the second is a bigoted bill preventing people from using the toilet. Pretending to be transgender would not make someone more comfortable using the toilet. It would only create problems, just like what would happen if all trans people suddenly started using the bathrooms that corresponded with our designated birth sexes. The idea that this is somehow better for the public is nonsense. The birthers just use that "logic" to try and stop us from using public bathrooms entirely.

Part Five: The "Why the Hell Are We Talking About This?" Chicken or Egg Debate

The idea that this is a stupid topic to constantly talk about exists on both sides of the equation. Who is to blame for all this talk of toilets, the transgender population or those who make the laws to oppress us? The more important question might be, where are we supposed to make our water?

The answer to this question reveals the whole truth. You see, a bathroom conspiracy theorist might say that transgender people can use designated single stall toilets that are supposedly available in all public or government-owned areas. This is a dog-whistle largely because there's no solution for the cases where there aren't any single stall toilets. Public buildings can be pretty old. You get a few far right politicians and media personalities who will outright say that transgender people should be forced to use the public bathroom that corresponds with their designated birth sex, but not too many. That rallying cry is usually reserved for the internet, where the cloak of anonymity protects the birther.

The question presents itself again: Where are we supposed to make our water?

We talk about this topic because people press forward with these stupid bathroom laws without offering anything that might placate this bigoted act in a first world country to people who might otherwise not really care about this issue. People care because it strips people of the very basic dignity that has defined first world countries since the Romans installed plumbing. You don't want to let us pee. Every last person who supports these bills should be forced to go on record and say those words.

Part Six: Who's Got a Ticket to Ride?

From a practical standpoint, the obvious must be asked. How exactly is this supposed to work? How does the government expect to keep those pesky transgender people out of the bathroom?

Cameras are a big no, for obvious reasons. Turning public restrooms into actual peepshows is probably not a good idea. Other countries charge money to use public toilets. Problem is that currency and coin slots are not exactly programmed with gender tests.

A TSA style pat-down security force would work. It would also be highly invasive and quite expensive. People needing to use the bathroom would be required to have their genitals prodded to make sure they had the right equipment. If that sounds like an extreme example, well, the bathroom laws are extreme bills. TSA agents aren't at airports to screen for transgender people. They're looking for bombs. The stakes here seem to be a little bit lower, though you wouldn't hear that from any of the people championing these bills.

Self-policing seems to be the preferred method of enforcement for these people who feel that the bathrooms bills are necessary enough for public safety, but will not go as far as to implement actual security that offers the kind of protection the politicians feel that the non-trans population needs. This too, is highly problematic. Imagine the untrained eye in search of those transgender people trying to breach the invisible perimeter on their way to the toilet. Kind of looks like a peep show.

Imagine someone trying to carry out a citizen's arrest because a transgender person used a public bathroom. This scenario seems likely to end in violence as soon as any bystander found out what was going on. This is bound to happen given the public's disdain for bathroom bills as a whole.

The question must then be asked again: How is this rule supposed to be enforced?

Part Seven: Give Me Trans-free Toilets or Give Me Death!

Remember when Republicans hated pointless government rules? Or at least pretended to with that picture of the snake that urges you not to step on it. "Don't tread on me," while I'm on my way to pee! Maybe they didn't mind the rules after all.

I guess the obvious question to pose for any proposed new rule for any circumstance is, is this really necessary? Is this issue really so much of a problem that we need to make a bathroom bill about it? Texas is moving forward with one even after seeing the backlash that North Carolina faced, complete with Governor McCrory's failed re-election bid. To Texas politicians, the answer must be yes, at least for enough of them.

"Is it necessary?" is a yes or no question. We can gather that to at least some people, the answer is yes. "Why is it necessary?" is just as important to ask. There should be a reason since it's been a while since we modified the old bathroom system. Our country used to have four bathroom options, taking race into consideration for reasons far more disgusting than these modern bathroom bills.

It is sad that we've been down the road before as a country, talking of liberty, but acting on bigotry. The question of "why is it necessary?" must be asked again, if only to observe the silence that follows. There is no good reason. If there is, let's hear it. Must be good, if we need a new rule. Republicans sure want the country to think they hate new rules and regulations, while doing everything in their power to demonstrate the opposite.

Part Eight: The Trouble with Solutions

Here's a question I love posing to proponents, or

sympathizers, of the bathroom bills. Granted, I've yet to encounter a single woman in favor of the bill, though the advocates always toss around the "we have to stop men using women's toilets," rallying cry. Ted Cruz loves that one.

Why do you want us in your bathrooms?

Isn't it kind of weird? All those male politicians in North Carolina and Texas who fight so hard to compel trans people to use the same bathrooms as them. Why do they want us to be forced to be in there while they take dumps?

This question often makes conservative people feel uncomfortable, as if it suggests a kind of fetish. Maybe there is something to that. It's not as if there have been many legitimate reasons offered. Perhaps there are more than a few nefarious ones. Transgender porn is pretty popular. Someone's got to be watching it.

There is a reason people don't like answering that question in front of actual transgender people. It forces the birthers to put a face on the abstract concept they love to use as a punching bag. It's awkward to think of an actual transgender person being forced to use the bathroom that corresponds to their birth sex because the image looks wrong. It is wrong. Transwomen have no place in men's bathrooms and transmen have no place in women's bathrooms.

Part Nine: What About the Actual Assaults?

The focus on transgender people's imaginary role in bathroom assaults can make it easy to forget that sexual crimes do happen in public places. Sex offenders may not dress up as members of the opposite sex before committing their heinous acts, but those acts are committed. It is not okay.

It is difficult to design laws that prevent crimes such as murder and sexual assault, which have been going on since before human beings started writing laws down. Most people know these actions are wrong already. There are things society can do to reduce the number of crimes that occur, but human beings are never going to stop doing bad things to each other. That is a fact, even if we don't have to accept it. We can always fight to change our reality.

The exact laws dealing with sexual assault and the subsequent handling of sex offenders varies from state to state. There is always more that a state can do to prevent sex crimes from happening within its borders.

Despite their frequent cries to the contrary, politicians have rarely demonstrated an ability to walk and chew gum at the same time. If they are focusing their time on bathroom bills against transgender people, chances are they're not doing much else on the sexual assault prevention front. They shouldn't be allowed to pretend that they care about the public.

Part Ten: It's a Public Bathroom, Not a Spa Paradise

The previous parts of this long saga all touch on one central idea. Public bathrooms are not fun places to be. They're often dirty. They almost always smell. You wouldn't want to hang out in them, even if they offered cucumber water.

Transgender people don't like them any more than anyone else, even the ones that actually correspond with our gender identities. We don't walk inside public bathrooms looking to start a book club or to look at people's private parts. We go in there to do our business, preferably as quickly as possible. Then we leave.

That's all there is to it. Pretending otherwise is wrong. We are not sexual deviants. We just want to use the bathroom in peace. Why is that so wrong?

ALTERNATIVE FACTS ABOUT TRANSGENDER PEOPLE

1. **Your gender is defined at birth, by your private parts**
2. **All trans people who think otherwise are wrong, and likely mentally ill.**
3. **Doctors are also wrong (mental health typically not evaluated).**
4. **Any court that has ever changed a transgender person's birth certificate is wrong too.**
5. **Gender identity is something that the "Book of Science" knows a lot about, but not climate change.**
6. **You're not allowed to touch your private parts for any reason other than hygienic purposes.**
7. **Once married, only your spouse can touch you, strictly for reproduction.**
8. **God only loves LGBT people if they remain chaste for life.**

9. **Transgender people have turned bathrooms into warzones resembling** *Mad Max: Fury Road.*
10. **The only three sins are heresy, sodomy, and rock & roll**

A WORLD WITHOUT THE CLOSET

Imagine a world where people weren't taught to subconsciously repress their own identities. A mind unburdened with the weight of illusion. A winning proposition for everyone involved, so it would seem.

Coming out of the closet feels liberating because you no longer have to carry all that crap around with you, in your mind, wherever you go. This kind of language makes the closet sound like a horrible place, which it is. Unfortunately, for many people, it is also necessary to spend some quality time inside, if just to figure shit out in peace, without the noise of the outside world.

The role of the closet has changed over the years. Coming out, or simply being out, is certainly easier in a more general sense given that society is, as a whole, more accepting of the LGBT community than it has been in the past. This does not change the fact that many LGBT youth have to stay in the closet for fear of their personal safety or that many people will still take punitive actions against LGBT people just for being who they are.

Imagine a world without that. Hard, isn't it? Not just

because it's hard to imagine a world without homophobia and/or transphobia, but also because it is literally difficult to visualize an abstract concept of that magnitude. But it's nice to think about.

People hate the closet because it takes a lot of energy to remain there. You can actually test this out for yourself, even if you aren't a member of the LGBT community. Go inside an actual closet and stay there. Even if you bring your phone or snacks or *War & Peace,* eventually you'll want to come out. Being in the figurative closet feels like that, including having the option to actually leave. Except you fear the seemingly endless dangers that lie on the other side of the door.

THERE IS NO "AVERAGE" TRANSITION

This concept can be tricky for some people, especially since transitioning itself is confusing enough already as it is. In case you are confused, I'll say it again.

There is no "average" transition.

Everyone moves at their own pace, with their own timelines, toward their own goals. Some people will have surgery. Others will not. There is no "right" way to do it, though there is one singular "wrong" way. That would be, staying in the closet.

The confusion is exacerbated by the sensitivity of the topic, though plenty of people see nothing wrong with asking another person about very intimate details of their life. People are entitled to their privacy, especially in instances as life-changing as transitioning, just as they are entitled to make their own decisions about their own lives.

IT ENDS WHEN IT ENDS

No set point in time. There are guidelines obviously, for when certain treatments become available, but no one gives you dates for when you "officially" become a member of your desired gender. This is simultaneously daunting and liberating.

Life is a process of learning and growth. It is important to remember that transgender people face an unusual learning curve in this realm, especially those of us who transitioned later in life. Many of us will literally face puberty twice. I don't know many people who have particularly fond memories of the process their first time around. Puberty is typically not a pleasant event that calls for a sequel.

There are countless subtleties to typical male/female behavior that people pick up on over the course of their lives. Transgender people get to view these through a different lens, shedding light on the value of such societal etiquette. In that regard, transitioning is never over.

CHANGES (TURN AND FACE THE STRANGE)

Do not succumb to an external sense of obligation to modify yourself, your being. Remove the weights which tie you down, but give each line a tug, to ensure that which is to be cut loose truly serves no benefit.

The world sees male and female as distinctly different beings. With this is mind, transitioning might seem like the stripping down of one existence, only to doll up another in its place. Everything kicked to the wayside, all of it. Even that which you cling to, as a part of your identity. This is not how life works.

The urge to resist is natural, to a certain extent, but it is not what you need. You need clarity, the kind that only a journey further down the rabbit hole will bring. The answers that will only come when you stop fighting and heed the dormouse's advice. Feed your head.

Embark on a voyage of liberation. The path before you might be scary, but fear not what you can control. You'll be surprised to learn how much is truly in your power.

DON'T CONCERN YOURSELF WITH "PASSING"

The biggest misconception people have about transgender people is that transitioning comes from a desire to wear the clothing of the opposite sex. Clothes are tools used in the expression of identity. Being transgender stems from a desire to express one's identity in all its forms, including that reflection in the mirror before any makeup or clothing goes on.

The term passing refers to successfully presenting as a member of your desired sex. The barometer for "success" is often gauged by being identified by a generic term specific to your gender, such as "miss" or "sir." It may seem like basic stuff, but it matters in a weird way, that little public acknowledgement that helps you reaffirm your own identity. Many of us have spent a great deal of time wondering if we'd ever achieve that teensy morsel of acceptance. It simultaneously is and isn't a big deal.

Transgender people must meet this standard just like anyone else, only with the added pressure of also being seen as dignified members of society, a bar that most working professionals are assumed to have met already, by token of their very presence in a place of commerce. Medical doctors prescribe various methods of HRT with the speed of transition taken into consideration, knowing full well that many people do have to look a certain way just to keep their livelihood. This is unfortunate, but also a reality that transgender people must face. Certainly better than many of the alternatives.

PASS ON YOUR OWN TERMS

Workplaces get to determine how their employers dress, within reason. The rest of your non-working identity is yours to craft. Transgender people naturally have a different relationship to the male/female binary than the cisgender population, but neither is forced to live under its claustrophobic umbrella.

You don't have to change at all really. Change is a magical, yet daunting component of the trans experience. *Pretty Woman* illustrated the immense power clothes hold over perspective. An obsession with fashion might point to an unhealthy preoccupation with material goods, but we should not forget the massive transformative abilities that simple garments can have.

Your name is also a factor in passing. You don't have to change it. I didn't. That comes with some added confusion, but not changing your name does not mean you fail the transgender test. There is no test.

You don't have to throw your old clothes away if you don't want to. Definitely keep the comfortable stuff. Don't be afraid of the idea that wearing old clothes signals hesitation on your part. They're yours and presumably something that either you or someone you loved paid for. Clothes do not define your identity. The stuff on the inside is supposed to be what counts. Middle schoolers hear that stuff a lot, but it is worth repeating again. Too often we forget the lessons learned that are worth remembering.

Passing is a concept that is supposed to bring comfort, offering the kind of simple acceptance that people can take for granted. An acknowledgement from the outside world that you are the person you've always thought you were. In reality, it often serves the opposite function from supplying comfort.

Passing is a fluid standard with endless

interpretations. This can breed anxiety for people worried about every little detail of their appearance. It is no different from being nervous before a date, spending long periods of time scanning yourself in the mirror for even a tiny imperfection. A dangerous activity, for no one is perfect.

STOP ASKING US ABOUT OUR PRIVATE PARTS (OR OTHER SURGERIES)

Can you think of an instance where it would be appropriate to go up to a person and ask them about potential surgeries they might be considering? This is often a touchy subject even for family members, yet the general population often feels perfectly comfortable asking transgender people about our plans for our private parts. The discussions often end up sounding like a person asking what accessories you plan to buy for your *American Girl* doll.

It is not really that hard to understand why someone would ask. It is an interesting subject. The line of questioning is invasive, but less presumptuous than simply asking a cisgender person if they plan to have any work done later in life. All transgender people have "work done," even if it's just on the inside.

We get it, you're curious. Problem is, these are objectifying questions regarding personal decisions. It is not appropriate casual conversation talk. Elizabeth Bennet would certainly not have approved of Mr. Darcy asking such questions of guests at a ball. Nor should you.

This line of questioning is becoming less socially acceptable as time goes on. A certain talk show host got in trouble for asking too many questions about a transgender woman's private parts. Surgeries represent a small part of the transgender experience and do not factor in to every single transition. Questions that focus on them are not only insensitive, they suggest a broader importance that just isn't true. We're not cars going in for new stereo systems.

If you're in doubt as to whether or not a question is inappropriate, here's a helpful tip. Ask yourself if you would feel comfortable asking that question to a cisgender person. Generally speaking, we as a society don't go around asking people about their private parts. They're called private for a reason.

BE SEEN

Transgender actors are marginalized for reasons that make no sense. You might think it was because there aren't too many transgender roles, but this really shouldn't be much of a problem. Can you think of a single show that spent any amount of time on cisgender people's gender identities?

Being transgender is not the only interesting, or distinctive trait about any of us. Transgender people can play any role, because fictional characters do not come with full backstories. Even if they were real people, the performance merely represents a reinterpretation of historical facts. Not a bit by bit recreation.

It's not as if this is a problem unique to transgender people. Minority groups face the same senseless discrimination. Hollywood has this belief that a certain type of person is the right kind of person to put in front of the camera. Talent matters. That isn't naïve either. The pretty faces fade if they can't keep your attention for longer than it takes to walk past their billboard on the Sunset strip. There are plenty of drop dead gorgeous transgender people to put up there too.

BELIEVE IN YOURSELF

That may sound like crappy advice to tell someone with self-esteem or confidence issues. I don't say it in the "magic words" sense that you hear in inspirational sports movies. More like the theme song to the long running children's series *Arthur*.

Let believing in yourself be your place to start. Transitioning is your chance to begin again, from the damage caused by years of holding it all back. Spend time crafting the image you want the world to see. Try out new looks to see what works and what doesn't.

That image should be your guide to passing, nothing else. The other standards are too problematic, and in many cases, impossible to meet. You'll never know if you've truly met someone's standards. Do yourself a favor, don't try.

THE "ONCE MALE" SPORTS ADVANTAGE

This is one of those tricky myths, because it makes a lot of sense when you first think about it. People say trans-women have an advantage in sports because of their "male build," or some similar terminology. If you hear that, it can definitely appear sensible. You just need to have a basic awareness that men are, on average, stronger than women.

Why is that? That answer is easy. Hormones.

Remember the big steroid controversy in baseball? That one acronym that kept getting tossed around. HGH. Also known as, human growth hormone. Key word being, hormone.

You know what baseball players don't do? They don't try to line their skeletons with liquid adamantium like Wolverine of the *X-Men*. Granted, you might think that comparison is ridiculous on account of the fact that Wolverine is a fictional comic book character, but baseball is a billion-dollar industry. If stuff like that really worked, people would try it. Hormones are where the real juice comes from.

If you'd prefer a real world example, the guidelines set by the International Olympic Committee regulate trans-gender athletes by hormone levels, not bone density or body build. It's not for a lack of ability to measure it either. Hormones affect bone density. We think the "male build" matters, because it makes sense visually in our heads. Lots of things do. That's why we do things called fact-checking and research to make sure the mental image actually checks out in reality.

The one about the "trans advantage" doesn't really check out. Testosterone is a powerful hormone. Transwomen don't like it. Without it, it doesn't seem likely that any of us will have a serious shot at Barry Bonds' home run record. Oh well. Happiness is a decent consolation prize.

THE CHOICE FALLACY

Transgender people cannot choose to be trans. We also cannot choose to not be trans, which is not the same as choosing not to transition. We are who we are and no amount of acceptance or denial can change the raw components that make up our individual identity.

I often joke that if I could choose, I would choose to not be trans. I say that not because I hate myself or that I regret transitioning, but because it would be the sensible choice. If I was presented with the option of either taking pills for the rest of my life, or not taking pills for the rest of my life, I would pick the latter option. I imagine most people would.

This is no different from any hypothetical involving being able to change any detail about yourself. Your hair color, height, breast size, length of your index finger, and so on. I imagine there are very few people who would honestly not change a thing about themselves if given the option.

Some might say that stating I would prefer to not be trans is dangerous, as if it suggests something is wrong with being trans. This couldn't be further from the truth. I love the fact that we embrace who we are, in spite of the immeasurable hardships that come with that choice. The choice to embrace yourself, to be happy. There is nothing better.

NO REGRETS

None whatsoever. It can be hard to believe. Some degree of regret, or longing for the old way of life, might even be healthy to a certain extant. I've never felt any.

The birthers like to claim that sizable percentages of the transgender population regret transitioning, usually referring to transgender individuals who have undergone surgical procedures. There are no serious studies that support this claim. There are plenty that have been conducted across the world that suggest the opposite. One study even reported that zero people regretted transitioning.[10]

The decision to transition takes a lot of thought. Mostly because it literally can't be made on a whim. Even trying HRT for a couple weeks can have lifelong repercussions. The subject of regret is perhaps the one area where the painfully long process of transitioning serves to our benefit. Very few of us regret transitioning because we've been aware of the risks for a very long time. We know what we're getting into. It's what we signed up for.

WE'VE THOUGHT ABOUT THIS (A LOT)

That distinction is important, as the general public discourse offers little evidence that many of the people who choose to "join the conversation" have actually sat down and thought about this stuff for any period of time long enough to form a substantive opinion. This short duration often gives people a sense that they are now experts on this subject. Ideas like "your gender is defined at birth" seem logical because those are words that a person can hear and understand as something that makes sense as a sequence of words.

There was a point where Aristotle's thoughts on gravity seemed to make sense. The idea that the sun revolved around the earth seemed pretty sound before Copernicus came along. If we're here and the sun moves, perhaps the sun moves around the earth! Obviously that's not how it works, but it took humanity a pretty long time to figure that one out.

Transgender people do not know why we are transgender. The unanswerable "why" isn't as important as the practical "is." We can work with the latter. Many of us are not that concerned with the former.

The lack of clarity on the former does not necessarily diminish its value as something to think about. This stuff is a big deal and comes with life-changing consequences. The "what-if" scenarios presented by people who don't spend much time thinking about transgender issues do not provide much value to the general discussion. Chances are, a transgender person has already considered that bright innovation on identity you may have thought up in line at Starbucks.

Which sounds obnoxious to say, except being transgender means that people can feel comfortable coming up to you to share these thoughts that they've often just thought up, or ask you questions about your private parts. Sometimes these conversations are productive while other times they're just unproductive debates on a subject where only one side has actual stakes in the game. It can be very frustrating to be on that side.

I mention this only because you may encounter a transgender person who doesn't want to talk about transgender issues with you. They could be being rude, but they also might just not want to talk about it. We've thought about this a lot already.

THE TERMINOLOGY WAR

Words are valuable. We know this. We use a combination of twenty-six different letters to communicate. Words evolve over time, like the slurs once used against LGBT people that are no longer acceptable to utter in everyday life.

Transgender people face backlash over words every day. Much of this relates to pronouns. Simple words that people fight over. Let's take a look.

Part One: The They/Them Singular Pronoun

The English language lacks a singular personal third person pronoun for non-binary people. They/them have been used as alternatives. This is either not a big deal or the end of civilization, depending on whom you ask.

I hate to burst the word police's bubble, but "they" has always been used to refer to singular nouns. Usually in an abstract sense to refer to a person of an unknown gender, like "Someone left their coat. I don't know what they were thinking." It stands to reason that using it to refer to specific, identifiable people, does not add a strenuous burden to anyone's life.

To play devil's advocate for a second, we should at least consider what the "they/them" singular pronouns mean. Words previously used for plural purposes are now being redefined. Pronouns are meant to make life easier. Changing a major element of what pronouns mean in the English language is kind of a big deal, even if it is not, in fact, the end of the world.

There are those who will ask the question, why should the entire population be forced to accept this change on behalf of a small segment of the transgender population? That question does seem fair enough to ask, except for one problem.

This isn't an either/or type scenario. The words aren't changing their meaning for the entire population. Just those few people. In a broader sense, this does slightly shift the meaning of the words away from their dominant status as plural pronouns, but they have always served singular purposes as well. This change really is not the end of the world.

"Why can't they (singular, or plural) pick a new word?"

I don't know. It would be easier if non-binary people all settled on "ze" or something similar and "they/them" could go on being strictly plural. It's not about ease. It's about comfort.

Part Two: Why Cisgender Matters (It's Not the "Default Setting")

Some people hate the term cisgender, which refers to people whose gender identity corresponds with the sex they were designated at birth. They hate this term because it applies to all people outside of the trans spectrum. For people who are skeptical of trans people already, this label seems unnecessary. They would prefer the term "normal people," or something similar, that reflects their assumed status as the ruling class. To them, we're the aberration, which is why we get the new terminology.

I don't love the term cisgender. It is a clunky word to say out loud. It has not been used in non-scientific conversation for very long. It is, however, important that the term exists.

There needs to be a term that notes the distinction between trans people and non-trans people. We can't just have transgender people and "everyone else," even if people can understand what "everyone else" refers to in that context. There are other contexts where it wouldn't be as applicable. Best to have an actual term and not a vague generality.

White people account for around 73% of America's total population according to the most recent census.[11] We don't refer to white people strictly as "people" when comparing them to other racial demographics. The supermajority doesn't get to be the "default setting."

There is not a default term for transgender people either. You may have heard the terms "transgenders" or "transgendered" used before in the media or in everyday life. Some people do not like those terms, especially "transgenders," as the absence of the word people reminds many of us that there are plenty of individuals out there who do not see us as people. Like cisgender, there is no consensus as to which term is the right one to use, which is perfectly okay. Life is not measured by consensus opinions.

People don't actually have to use the term cisgender. The fact that it exists is enough, recognizing that there are many forms of gender and there are terms to refer to each one, even the one that includes the vast majority of the population. Transgender people are not anomalies. Just another flavor of humanity. We have our words that describe us, just like everyone else. Even the cisgender people.

Part Three: Drafting The Word Police

Once again the question of who gets to decide this stuff presents itself. And yet again, the answer is the public, which of course gets in the way of the "needs of the many vs. the needs of the few" debate. If this change is only something that applies to a small group of people, why would the masses hop aboard such a silly proposition?

The answer: basic decency.

It is true that calling a single person "they or them" requires more brain power if you're not otherwise used to doing that. It goes against the programming of the subconscious, which previously applied different pronouns to serve that singular meaning. It can be frustrating, even annoying, but consider the person at the receiving end of these new pronouns.

A person who chooses "they/them" does so because they felt most comfortable with those pronouns. This person looked at the available options, including the gendered singular pronouns, and they decided that they did not like them. They like "they/them" instead. You may not like that, but they do and they're the ones who get to decide.

It is however, completely up to you whether or not you wish to associate yourself with someone who uses "they/them" pronouns. You can certainly choose to avoid people who prefer those words to other words, ignoring that everyone likes to be referred to in a certain way.

Do you know someone who goes by an unusual pronunciation of their name? "Davvveeeed" rather than the way you'd say David if I hadn't spelt it that way. Or surnames with different pronunciations in different cultures, like Benoit. We as a society tend to respect this, even if people with those names want to be referred to in a way that's different from what we're used to. Again, this really just falls under the category of human decency. It's not *that* big of a deal.

The public is increasingly accepting of this whole concept. It will continue to evolve as time goes on. Is that because the public likes the repurposing of pronouns, or simply does not want to be a collective asshole about it? I'm not sure the answer to that really matters.

Part Four: The Politically Correct Fallacy

Despite its name, political correctness is a controversial concept. Its boundaries shift over time, causing endless wars over where we should set the partitions. Gender neutral pronouns are seen as "P.C." A lot of people do not care for them for that very reason.

Calling people by their preferred terminology should be seen as a decent way to treat an individual, not as indicative of politically correct culture gone astray. One could try to argue that the individual is not really the problem, only indicative of its larger ramifications. This kind of rationale makes the case that one person choosing their pronouns leads to a world where we all ask for each other's pronouns upon first contact, something that is starting to happen in college classrooms and in email signatures.

While the fear of this abstract future possibility is overstated in almost all cases, trepidation toward a reality where variations of "Hi, my name is <insert name here>. My pronouns are <insert pronouns here>" become the standard human greeting is at least something we can comprehend. There are people out there who are not bigots, who also don't think that this is necessary for this country at this point in time. Again, we should remember that trans/non-binary people only make up a small portion of the overall population.

Trouble is, we don't live in that reality. That isn't the standard greeting. There are however individuals who do wish to be referred to by pronouns that are outside the ones you might normally assign for them. That idea is not a sign of political correctness wreaking havoc on the moral fiber of our nation. Those who suggest otherwise are likely trying to use it to cover some other feelings they're not too proud of.

Part Five: On Misgendering

Misgendering is another fairly clunky term that opens itself up to ridicule. What it refers to, people being referred to by the wrong gender terminology, is not a laughing matter. It is an act often committed for hateful purposes, when birthers use your birth pronouns to try and delegitimize you.

Sometimes, however, it isn't.

People slip. They use the wrong word. Instinctively. Pronouns are tricky. They're used to make life easier. That's why people use he/she/they/them/ze to refer to people rather than solely using proper nouns. The subconscious is often very set in its ways.

Mistakes happen. It hurts when transgender people are called by improper terminology because that action signals a rejection of the identity we've worked so hard to achieve, even if it wasn't intentional. That's the power of words.

I've slipped many times and called myself by my former pronouns or used slang terminology like "man" or "dude" to refer to myself. It's a habit. It doesn't happen as much anymore, but it does take some getting used to. I didn't transition for the purpose of new pronouns, though it always feels nice to hear the new ones said out loud. Simple courteous acts mean a lot to people who have taken a lot of heat just for trying to feel okay.

You don't have to sweep mistakes under the rug and pretend they didn't happen, but it is important to consider the intent of the person who misgendered you. Often, it is just a mistake. As the recipient of hate speech on more than a few occasions, I can definitely say I know what that sounds like. It doesn't sound like the slip of "he," followed by a sincere sounding apology.

Correct people who misgender you. Don't feel like it's something you shouldn't care about if you do care. You have a right to be called by the proper terminology, just like anyone else.

Part Six: The "Cute Terms" for Male Fashion Trends

Terms such as "man bun," "man purse," "guyliner," "meggings," and the new "romp-him" (romper) have entered the American lexicon. These terms refer to new fashion trends involving men wearing garments or using grooming regiments once thought of as exclusive to women. The term metrosexual comes to mind. While they may be amusing to read, and certainly to say out loud, they are dangerous roadblocks preventing the collapse of the binary.

That notion might also make you laugh. Think about it. What purpose do these unnecessary labels serve, other than to single out that these stylistic choices go against the grain? Eyeliner is applied to people's eyelids. Leggings are worn by people who have legs. The gendered associations exist solely as social constructs. Men used to wear leggings all the time in the middle ages. Probably would have shopped at Sephora too, if there had been one at the faire.

Society draws attention to the unusual, only to mock it. These terms tell us that individuality only matters if it does not threaten the longstanding pillars of masculinity. So much for being unique.

MEN USED TO HAVE LONG HAIR. JESUS, HERCULES, JOHN LENNON, JON SNOW

"Man buns" have received more backlash than any of these other trends. There are countless articles on the internet calling for their imminent demise. The end of 2015 in particular saw several publications calling for the new year to bring with it plenty of haircuts. Clip-on "man buns" were even designed to cash in on the popularity, giving short-haired people the chance to experience what it feels like to let your hair flow in the breeze.

Why? It's not as if there's a single costume drama that does not have at least one attractive man with long hair. Brad Pitt and Johnny Depp, two of only four people to win *People's* "Sexiest Man Alive" multiple times, have lived large portions of their lives with long hair. It is safe to gather then, at least some people do enjoy long hair on men.

The "man bun" phenomenon seeks to castigate those men who wish to avoid the barber through trivialization and shame. Legitimate reasons, like personal grooming preferences, are tossed out the window in favor of a mob mentality, broadcast by those fashion writers who use their bully pulpits to dictate public fashion policy.

Long hair is neither a bad thing nor a trend. Men have had long hair since before the dawn of scissors. Don't listen to the voices who mock long hair with stupid terms. They're probably just jealous that they, or their boyfriends, can't rock the flow. Plenty of very attractive men have. So did Jesus. That should tell us all we need to know.

CELEBRITIES DO NOT DEFINE US

It should not surprise anyone that there are not that very many transgender celebrities. Our acceptance in mainstream culture is relatively new. This leads to scenarios where the behavior of certain celebrities can be seen as representative of our larger community. Assumptions form, as if the actions of individuals ever serve as accurate indicators as to the normal conduct of an entire minority group.

No singular person speaks for all of us. Or any of us. Retweets do not equal endorsements. Though it may seem that way, celebrities are not our democratically-elected representatives. They're just people.

This may seem obvious, except for all the times trans people are asked to speak about the broad sentiments of the LGBT community. People do assume that certain celebrities represent us all. We can't be sure why, but it could be because they don't know that many transgender people. Or any at all. It is easy to think of a single celebrity as representative of an entire minority group if that celebrity represents your only experience with that group.

Some transgender celebrities face criticism in the public eye. I'm not going to name names. Criticism levied against transgender people should not be seen as detrimental toward our fight for equality for one simple reason. No single person defines us. People are criticized all the time. We tend to not like the idea of assigning broader ramifications for people's actions to others belonging to their race, gender identity, or sexual orientation. That's called discrimination.

STOP THE SCAPEGOATING

The bathroom bill and the proposed military ban on transgender soldiers do more than suggest problems where there are none. They point the finger at a marginalized group that has more than enough bullshit to deal with already. Why?

It's easy to pick on the people perceived to be toward the bottom of the social totem poll. Some people might even enjoy it, since it reassures them that someone else is less than them. Humanity finds strange ways to entertain itself. Just look at what's on TV at three in the morning.

Scapegoating is an easy thing to do when you can

attack your enemies in the abstract sense, never having to face the people you hurt. This is another realm where our lack of visibility serves to our disadvantage. Remorse is absent when there's no one there to tell you that your actions actually affected someone. It's why online trolls rarely behave the same way in public. They know they couldn't tolerate the guilt of having to spout their hate face to face. Cowards.

Transgender people don't need this crap. Cut it out. There are real consequences to this bullshit that often passes as "lively debate."

This is not the same as saying there can't be a reasonable debate on LGBT issues or that nothing negative can ever be said about transgender people because it might make us sad. Only that the current crop of topics, like chromosomes and toilets, hasn't yielded much in the way of substantive discussion. We're more than capable of handling adult conversations. Is anyone else?

WE ARE NOT A WEDGE ISSUE

Americans are not as divided as our politicians want us to think. This just doesn't make for a very compelling electoral narrative. This is why we have wedge issues, big complex problems that only seem to come up when politicians express their individual abstract solutions that always seem to disappear once the winner is sworn in. American politicians like wedge issues so that they do not have to actually do anything in order to get re-elected.

Politics often rewards the loudest voice in the room. It always gets heard. There is a large enough voting bloc to reward anti-LGBT positions, even if a majority of Americans support gay marriage and are opposed to transgender bathroom bills. Though most Americans do not favor turning back the clock on our civil liberties, we have to keep talking about the issue in order to appease those loud voices who don't wish to be quiet. Those voices like to give money to politicians.

Treating LGBT rights as a wedge issue also essentially prevents us from fully participating in a key element of American democracy. Putting the state of contemporary politics aside, America's electoral system was unique when it was founded because it gave people a choice of who to cast their vote for. Many countries still do not allow their citizens to participate in the political process.

Do LGBT people really live in a two party system? While an eternal optimist might point to free will and voting ballots that offer many choices, beyond the standard red/blue fare, let's not kid ourselves. LGBT people will never truly have options when one party has a disgusting record on basic civil rights and a willingness to play footsy with birthers, both past and present. The odds of a third party rising up to national prominence seems higher than the Republican Party ever broadly acknowledging that gay people are not responsible for the decline of America.

Again this represents an area where the people can change the landscape. Not now, but someday. Politics may seem like an endless cycle of bureaucratic nonsense and that cycle will continue. Decades from now, the good ol' boys might see the error in their ways, acknowledging that all people have a right to the basic civil liberties our Constitution was founded on. Support for LGBT rights has grown exponentially over the past ten years. We the people can force the next ten years to continue that rapid growth. It's about damn time.

WOULD WE HAVE TRANSGENDER PEOPLE WITHOUT THE BINARY?

An unanswerable question. It is fun to think about, even if we'll never learn the answer. The binary can be torn down, but its memory will remain. A world without the binary is still a world where it once belonged. Transgender people know our own identities because of it, a frame of reference to guide you down the proper path.

Just from personal experience, the idea that transgender people would continue to transition without a gender binary is supported by the effectiveness of HRT. My body was not a huge fan of testosterone. The binary is not to blame for that.

The binary takes heat for the rules it arbitrarily enforces, even as the world evolves past its dated ideology. The world would be a better place without it, but I don't deny it served some value in my life. It allowed me to see where I was and where I should be. It protects its rules without ever having to explain them. With that in mind, it does not seem as daunting a foe. We see the way it governs the world and we can reject it, one barrier at a time.

WHERE DOES "CROSS-DRESSING" FIT IN?

Many trans people, myself included, dislike the term cross-dressing. It is often mistakenly used as a synonym for being transgender, which is pretty strange considering there's a clear known difference between the two. Cross-dressers like wearing the clothes of the opposite sex. Transgender people have a different gender identity from their designated birth sex. It's kind of like assuming that someone who likes *Grey's Anatomy* wants to be a doctor. Maybe that particular choice of television program is an indicator, but you wouldn't bet on it.

Cross-dressing relies on poking fun at the binary. Why else would a man wearing women's clothes and behaving in an effeminate manner be funny unless he, as a man, was not supposed to behave like that? Spelling out the humor makes it sound less amusing, though to be fair, there does not appear to be a big rush to remake *Some Like It Hot* or *Tootsie* either. Maybe people realized cross-dressing wasn't very funny after all.

We must address the pink elephant in the room. Men are inevitably singled out as cross-dressers far more than women, because men's fashion options are much more restrictive. There's no easy solution for this, except one that is potentially too toxic for the typical fragile male ego.

Wear women's clothes. Despite the name, they are not just for women. Does that sound ridiculous to you? It shouldn't, but if it does, let's take a look at why it might be worth considering.

BENEFITS OF FEMALE GARMENTS/FASHION

1. **Spanx are quite handy.**

The idea of affection for shapewear is a controversial subject. Some people regard the concept of fabric designed to keep every part of you sucked in like a sausage casing abhorrent. The problem with this logic is that it places comfort at the forefront of desire, when we know there are often other more important considerations that must be made.

People like to look good. Spanx, or other types of shapewear, help immensely on that front. They keep everything in! Nice smooth lines that anyone, or everyone, can appreciate.

Men love to play footsy with this topic. Spanx does have a line of menswear. Tank tops and boxer briefs designed to achieve the same objectives as the women's line. They are supposed to make you look thinner, or firmer, than you'd otherwise look if you weren't wearing a tight spandex undergarment.

I say fuck it. Wear the women's ones. The full body-suits, that really target the areas you're worried about. The reason the men's line looks different is not to tailor to the male body, but rather the male ego. The undershirts are never going to target the problem areas quite as well.

Men wear shapewear for a reason. We live in a super-ficial world. There's no point in half-assing the effort. No one will laugh because no one will see. Just wear the body-suit and be happy, as happy as anyone wearing something that tight can be.

2. **Makeup works.**

Why do people wear makeup? Cosmetic products enhance one's appearance. Why should these benefits be limited to one gender? Whose cheeks couldn't use a little blush?

Makeup can be a great confidence booster. It gives you control over the image your face presents to the outside world. Just like smiling, even when you're not happy. Makeup eases that burden, giving the world something else to turn its gaze toward. That kind of power can be wielded with an extra fifteen minutes in the bathroom (with practice).

Men already use concealer. They think we don't notice. It's useful. It conceals. Makeup can be used to express yourself as well. Those experiences should not be limited to women. Everyone should be free to be as colorful as they want to be.

I'm not suggesting that every man should run out to

Sephora to pick up a contour palette before spending five hours watching YouTube tutorials, but there's a reason people do that kind of stuff. It's fun to be able to transform yourself. If you don't believe me, try it.

3. Clothing is designed for body type.

There are different size charts for men and women, even though men and women both have waists and the same general composition that defines traits like height. There are obvious differences, but many of these are determined by size or height rather than one's gender. Bust size is a slight outlier, though probably not as much of one as men would like to admit.

Does tight clothing look better on women than men? If you think that's a problematic question, good. It is.

A world where clothes were designed for body type rather than gender would likely continue to produce trends that showed one gender still favoring one cut over another. This is not a bad thing. Body type still denotes some distinctions between the genders. It's just a better system to determine those differences. If something looks good on you, wear it. That should be your only consideration.

4. Underwear should be super comfortable.

Men's underwear often fails in this regard. Underwear is the most intimate layer of clothing. It shouldn't be itchy, scratchy, or any sensation short of divine. Men's underwear as a whole is not very comfortable.

What is the point of boxers? That's not a question we think about very often. It also doesn't have an obvious answer.

Some women's underwear is impractical for men, because clothes are designed for body type. Plenty of styles can accommodate the particulars of the male reproductive organs. It's not very hard to figure out which ones. Just hold them up and see!

It is important to again remember that no one can see. There are no "broader implications" for such a decision, despite the potential fears of the fragile male ego. Wear what makes you comfortable, which should in theory be the comfortable type of underwear. If you're miserable in life, take a look in your underwear drawer. Seeing too many boxers might not be a coincidence.

5. Men's clothes are boring.

I know many women hate being asked who they're wearing at the Oscars, but there's a reason people don't ask the men. A fine Italian suit represents the pinnacle of men's fashion, but as a whole the field lags far behind the women's in terms of possibilities. It's not even close.

Why not expand beyond the typical pants/jacket/shirt template? There's a reason men invest in fancy watches or cufflinks. They may look nice, but they also represent some of the few areas where men can truly individualize their wardrobes under the current societal guidelines.

Dresses completely change the game. They come in all different shapes and sizes, not just the boring "put your arms through the sleeves" variety. Some of them don't even have sleeves!

This notion might be ridiculous to you. You might think that men aren't "supposed" to wear dresses. Why not? What is the reason? Where do kilts fit in?

Men don't wear dresses because they don't wear dresses. That's not a very good reason. Now, some men don't want to wear dresses. A lack of desire is a slightly better reason, but the question of why still remains. Maybe you don't care enough to. Fine, but there are plenty of people out there who would like to, but feel they can't for that problematic reason called societal pressure. If you're one of those people, allow me to let you in on a little secret. There isn't a good reason. Just do it.

None of this is meant to be an attack on suits or jackets. Some of them look very sharp. There are just so many other possibilities out there to waste your life constantly returning to that same navy blue blazer. In women's fashion, that'd be considered a major faux pas. For good reason.

6. **Pockets are oppressive.**

From an abstract point of view, pockets are very useful. Pockets hold things, freeing your hands for more important duties, like playing on your phone or holding your Starbucks cup. Problem is, pockets don't hold very much.

Purses on the other hand, hold lots of stuff. Americans like stuff.

Think of your average American male leaving the house. What does he need? The three basic essentials of cell phone, wallet, and keys come to mind. All three of those might fit in a pocket, but that can be pretty bulky, forcing you to walk around with large lumps protruding from your thighs. The matter becomes more complex if a man is wearing skinny jeans. Money clips are not the answer.

Purses give you the option of putting those things, plus bonus treats, into one bag that you can sling over your shoulder. It makes sense. You don't have to cram them all into your pockets, leaving that space open for your hands if you're cold or stuck in a boring conversation.

You ever get hungry on the go, but don't want to carry around a backpack or a clunky briefcase? Can't put a Milky Way in your pocket unless you want it to melt in about five seconds. You can however, put a nougat-filled snack in a purse. Not so silly now, is it?

Men have tried this. There's the satchel, which is often mocked as a "man purse," in a similar fashion as the other feminine male fashion trends. I don't have as much sympathy for the satchel. Most satchels look pretty ugly. Indiana Jones is pretty much the only person who can pull one off, and even then, it didn't make the fourth movie any better. It's hard to argue that he wouldn't have looked better with a Louis Vuitton purse. Most people would.

Purses, on the other hand, are often very cute and come in colors other than brown or tan. Purses are literally too great for just one gender. Can you honestly think of a single reason why this isn't 100% accurate? I didn't think so.

7. **Men like this stuff.**

In addition to all the previous examples, think about Halloween costumes, "womanless" pageants, drag queens. Where does that desire come from? Simple, really.

It's fun.

Drag queens like dressing up. That's why *Ru Paul's Drag Race* is so much fun to watch. Everyone on the screen is having such a great time that the fun radiates through the fourth wall all the way to the viewer.

Men knew they'd be mocked for the "man bun" and went and did it anyway. Drag queens know the social stigmas floating out there every time they put their makeup on. There is a reason. Social etiquette has value in some sense, offering guiding principles as to how to conduct oneself in the world. It isn't very good at explaining, or justifying, its many contradictions.

Be fabulous, boys, if that's where your heart takes you. You'll enjoy it. Makes a hell of a lot more sense than the alternative. No fun for no reason is no good.

8. **This isn't silly nonsense.**

The tone of this section is undoubtedly lighter than pretty much everything else in this book. That does not mean that fashion discussions are not important or that this is nonsense. There are plenty of men who would adopt women's fashion trends if it were socially acceptable to do so.

It should be socially acceptable, for society cannot

explain why it is not. It's not going to lead to perverts or those other strange hypotheticals. We're just talking about clothes. Clothes that might look good on a lot of people, if only we let them.

Let's say it one more time: There is no good reason men shouldn't wear makeup or dresses. The binary has propped up dated fashion norms for far too long. Just another reason to tear it down!

WE ALL GET ONE CHANCE AT THIS THING CALLED LIFE

Imagine yourself decades from now looking back at your life, full of regret. An unfulfilled existence, devoid of that which your mind called for, defined by repression. How does that sound?

Despite the good words proclaimed from churches across the land, we have no guarantee of an afterlife. Only this one. It could be taken from any of us, at any time, for any reason. Disaster does not wait until you've lived a full life.

The people who claim that being transgender is a choice are right in one regard. Living freely as the person you were meant to be is, in fact, a choice. You can choose not to. The decision to transition reflects the time spent grappling with that difficult question:

Are you going to give yourself a real chance to be happy?

Our alarmingly high suicide rate reflects the number of people who didn't see a world where that could happen. The choice to live a repressed life may bring some happiness here and there, but it should not be considered a viable option. Those feelings of longing to be complete have a funny way of popping up when you least expect them.

Take your chance now. Don't become an old person filled with regret. Which isn't to say you should go and buy a bottle of estradiol off the internet because you think you might be trans, eager to live every last minute of your time left on earth as the person you think you might be.

Only to take care of yourself. Figure out who you are and what you need to be whole. We only get one shot as this thing called life, unless organized religion is actually on to something. Best to make it count.

YOU DON'T HAVE TO LIKE US

You, do not have to like trans people. Really. You may think you already know that, but it bears repeating.

Not liking someone is not the same as wanting to deny someone rights. Think back to the kindergarten classroom. You didn't have to like everyone, but that didn't mean you could go around pulling people's hair just because you didn't want to invite them to your birthday party.

I don't like the fact that some people want nothing to do with me because I'm transgender. I'm not going to let that inconvenient truth affect how I view this liberating journey of self-acceptance. They can't rain on my beautiful rainbow parade.

Think of a person you know who is obsessed with something that you don't particularly care for, possibly crocheting or Zumba. Chances are, you wouldn't want to spend much time with this person, if all they talked about is something that you're not interested in. This person is not someone you want to invite to your viewing party for *The Bachelor.*

Would you want to take their human rights away? Not in a metaphorical sense either. If given the option to literally make this person's life a living hell because they love crocheting, would you really want to do that? A hobby might not be the same as an identity, but neither is harming you.

A line is crossed when a dislike of an entire group turns into something broader, like government-sanctioned discrimination. Transgender people do not pose a threat to anyone just for being transgender. There is no legitimate reason to oppress us.

Live and let live, except in a real sense. Cute little phrases about loving each other lose their meaning when society picks and chooses how it wants to view morality. You don't have to like transgender people. That is not a good reason to try and deny us basic human dignity.

WE'RE NOT GOING AWAY

The trans-liberation movement has come too far to turn back. It won't happen. Deep down, everybody knows it. These efforts to delegitimize us or convince us that we're all somehow mistaken will inevitably fail, just like every other civil right's battle in this country. We don't even need an amendment, just a judge to tell the birthers to piss off.

What's the point of the fight? This question has been posed quite a few times over the course of this book, but it should be asked once more because it's pretty important. We're here. We're out of the closet, and we're never going back. Really. That isn't going to happen. The fantasy of the birthers will never come true.

Some people don't like that. Fine, but it is quite irrational to think there's anything that can be done to buck the tide of LGBT liberation. Also hateful. No one's forcing you to come to our Pride parades, even if most people look good in rainbow.

THIS WAR WILL NOT GO ON FOREVER

It sure seems that way, as countless other battles for civil rights wage on, decades after Amendments to our Constitution called for the end of this particularly foul brand of bullshit. The possibility that we may never achieve equal rights is as scary as it is depressing, but that kind of defeatism serves no purpose in the larger fight. We should not be hopeless either, for there have been many victories over even the past ten years.

Though the war for marriage equality wages on in certain parts of the country, the larger debate is settled. The Supreme Court has spoken. Public support for same sex marriage appears unlikely to ever dip below 50% again on the national level. Of course, none of this prevents future setbacks along the way, but any substantive effort to turn back the clock on LGBT rights will be met with swift fury and powerful resistance.

The word "gay" is no longer an accepted synonym for stupid. Celebrities can no longer use the word "faggot" on television without incurring punishment from either their employers or society at large. The Joint Chiefs of Staff rebuked President Trump's tweet calling for a ban on transgender military personnel. Progress is being made, even if many of us are frustrated by how long it has taken, for no obvious reason.

These changes add up over time. Society is actually pretty good at self-policing when it realizes that some things should not be tolerated in a public setting. It is just sad that this realization has taken longer than it needs to.

GO OUT AND CHANGE THE WORLD

You'd be surprised at how many tolerant people there are in the world when you go out and live in it, as your true self. The vast majority of humanity, in my experience. For all the evil out there in the world, all the bigotry and hate, people are still fundamentally good. I genuinely believe that.

The internet has benefited the transgender community in countless ways, serving as a vital tool for people who might otherwise have nowhere else to turn in periods of loneliness and isolation. It has also served as a very effective shield for people to spout hate speech without any real world experience with those they condemn.

There are ways to fix this.

I don't suggest that anyone try to publicly shower online trolls in flowers and glitter to melt their hearts of stone. That could be fun, but also potentially dangerous. We don't need to be "trans ambassadors" spreading the message that we're not actually the cause of the decline of America, despite what you might hear on talk radio.

But you should engage the world. Life's too short not to. It's a fun place, a lot of the time.

The people out there who have never interacted with a transgender person lack a frame of reference for the group the right constantly demeans. It helps to give them one through basic human conversation. Simple stuff. People acting as people. We use technology to shield ourselves, though that same shield can serve as a safe breeding ground for bigotry and hate. Humanity is pretty good at spreading love when it wants to. Look at the responses to any natural disaster.

In spite of these needless battles still being waged, I look to the future with optimism. We still have a long way to go on this journey for equality, and that's unfortunate. Doesn't change the fact that we've come so far already. So many bright and beautiful faces out and unafraid.

Our political climate might be more toxic than the Pripyat amusement park after Chernobyl, but now is still the best time to be alive for transgender people. I mean that. There's a lot of hate out there, but there's also a lot of love.

People do change the world. It may not always feel that way, because those tectonic shifts are best viewed in retrospect. There will come a day when we stop having pointless discussions over which groups should get to have the rights that we abstractly agree all people should be afforded, by right of our existence. There's a lot of other things worth talking about besides public bathrooms.

There is no doubt, even with that particular orange individual in the White House, that we live in the easiest time in America to be transgender. State laws and medical advances offer us protection and security that no previous era offered. This will continue to be the case as time moves forward, as long as we as a society do not look back.

You are loved. Just remember, because we all forget sometimes, to love yourself.

ACKNOWLEDGEMENTS

Thank you to my family, Mom, Dad, Colonel, Bibble, and Jorge for all their support throughout my transition.

I'd also like to thank my cover designer Robin Harper and my formatter Stacey Blake, who are always a treat to work with. Also many thanks to Toni Rakestraw for doing a great job combing over the manuscript.

Amy Bartelloni has been supportive of my transition since day one and has been my best friend in the chaotic world of publishing.

Special thanks to Tara Hattendorf for being a great friend and for helping to cite the court decisions used in this book.

A full list of people who have supported me in my various endeavors would take up a book of its own. The words of encouragement mean everything to me, especially on the days that aren't so fun. Thank you.

Lastly, thank you to all the transgender people out there, especially the ones who have paved the way for us to follow over the years. I am eternally grateful for the inspiration you provide me on a daily basis. Together, we will achieve a better tomorrow. For all those we've lost, you will not be forgotten.

ABOUT THE AUTHOR

Ian Thomas Malone is an author, transgender activist, and yogi from Greenwich, Connecticut. She is a graduate of Boston College, where she founded *The Rock at Boston College*. Ian enjoys glazed donuts, new wave music, and used bookstores. She lives in Long Beach, California.

NOTES

1 Obergefell v. Hodges, 135 S. Ct. 2584 (2015) www.supremecourt.gov/opinions/14pdf/14-556_3204.pdf

2 For further reading on Thomas(ine) Hall, I recommend this article. Vaughan, Alden T. "The Sad Case of Thomas(Ine) Hall." *The Virginia Magazine of History and Biography*, vol. 86, no. 2, 1978, pp. 146–148.

3 For further reading on Chevalier D'Eon, this article is recommended. Kates, Gary. "The Transgendered World of the Chevalier/Chevalière D'Eon." *The Journal of Modern History*, vol. 67, no. 3, 1995, pp. 558–594.

4 "The Constitution of the United States," Amendment 10.

5 The full fourth court ruling for G.G. v. Gloucester Cty. Sch. Bd., 853 F.3d 729 (4th Cir. 2017) can be found here www.ca4.uscourts.gov/Opinions/Published/161733R1.P.pdf

6 Phillips, Amber. "Is Split-Ticket Voting Officially Dead?" *The Washington Post*, WP Company, 17 Nov. 2016.

7 The full policy update by the World Health Organization can be found here www.who.int/bulletin/volumes/92/9/14-135541/en/

8 Flores, A.R., Herman, J.L., Gates, G.J., & Brown, T.N.T. (2016). *How Many Adults Identify as Transgender in the United States?* Los Angeles, CA: The Williams Institute.

9 Pullella;, Philip. "Pope Says Gender Theory Part of 'Global War' on Marriage, Family."*Reuters*, Thomson Reuters, 1 Oct. 2016.

10 Krege, S., Bex, A., Lümmen, G., Rübben, H.. "Male-to-Female Transsexualism: a Technique, Results and Long-Term Follow-up in 66 Patients." *BJU International.*, U.S. National Library of Medicine, Sept. 2001.

11 The full 2010 Census of Population and Housing summary can be found here https://www.census.gov/prod/cen2010/doc/dpsf.pdf

www.ingramcontent.com/pod-product-compliance
Lightning Source LLC
Chambersburg PA
CBHW060459280326
41933CB00014B/2791